Families

Deseret Book Company
Salt Lake City, Utah

Library of Congress Cataloging-in-Publication Data

Families.
     p.   cm.
   ISBN 0–87579–902–7
   1. Family—Religious life. 2. Mormons—Family relationships.
3. Child rearing—Religious aspects—Mormon Church. 4. Parenting—
Religious aspects—Mormon Church. 5. Parent and child—Religious
aspects. 6. Sociology, Christian (Mormon) 7. Mormon Church—
Doctrines. 8. Church of Jesus Christ of Latter-day Saints—Doctrines.
BX8643.F3F35   1994
248.4' 89332—dc20   94–12126
                                                                     CIP

Printed in the United States of America
10   9   8   7   6   5   4   3   2   1

Contents

Continue in Faith

PRESIDENT HOWARD W. HUNTER

General Authorities have the privilege of meeting and getting acquainted with members of the Church all over the world who have consistently lived good lives and raised their families in the influence of the gospel. These Saints have enjoyed the great blessings and comfort that can come from looking back as parents, grandparents, and great-grandparents over long and successful parenting efforts. Surely that is something each of us would like.

Nevertheless, there are many in the Church and in the world who are living with feelings of guilt and unworthiness because some of their sons and daughters have wandered or strayed from the fold. My remarks here are directed primarily to those mothers and fathers.

Conscientious parents try their best, yet nearly all have made mistakes. One does not launch into such a project as parenthood without soon realizing that there will be many errors along the way. Surely our Heavenly Father knows, when He entrusts His spirit children to the care of young and inexperienced parents, that there will be mistakes and errors in judgment.

For every set of parents there are many "first-time" experiences that help to build wisdom and understanding, but each such experience results from the plowing of new ground, with the possibility that errors might be made. With the arrival of the first child, the parents must make decisions about how to teach and train, how to correct and discipline. Soon there is the first day at school and the first bicycle. Then follows the first date of the first teenager, the first problem with school grades, and possibly, the first request to stay out late or the first request to buy a car.

It is a rare father or mother indeed who travels the difficult path of parenting without making errors along the way, especially at these first-time milestones when experience and understanding are somewhat lacking. Even after the parent has gained experience, the second-time and third-time occurrences of these milestones are sometimes not much easier to handle, nor do they come with much less chance of error.

What more challenging responsibility is there than working effectively with young people? Numerous variables determine the character and the personality of a child. It is probably true that parents are, in many or perhaps most cases, the greatest influence in shaping the life of a child, but sometimes other influences are also very significant. No one knows the degree to which heredity influences lives, but certainly brothers and sisters, friends and teachers, neighbors and Scoutmasters have significant effects.

We know, too, that the influences on a child are not restricted to heredity or to people; certainly, things in the physical surroundings will have their effect—such as the house and the playthings, the yard and the neighborhood. Playgrounds and basketballs, dresses and cars—or the lack of these—all have their influence on the child.

One must conclude that—with the multitude of influences and the innumerable decisions, each with so many alternatives to consider and evaluate—even though parents strive to choose wisely, an unwise choice will sometimes be made. It is almost impossible always to say and do the right thing at every point along the way. I think we would agree that as parents we have made mistakes that have had a negative effect on the attitude of the child or on the child's progress. On the other hand, parents usually do the right thing or make the right decision under the circumstances, yet sons and daughters often have negative responses to right or correct decisions.

If a parent has made what could be considered an error—or, on the other hand, has never made a mistake, but still the lamb has wandered from the fold—in either case there are several thoughts I would like to share with you.

First, such a father or mother is not alone. Our first parents knew the pain and suffering of seeing some of their children reject the teachings of eternal life. (See Moses 5:27.) Centuries later Jacob came to know of the jealousy and ill feelings of his older sons toward his beloved Joseph. (See Genesis 37:1–8.) The great prophet Alma, who had a son named Alma, prayed at length to the Lord regarding the rebellious attitude of his son and no doubt was overwhelmed with concern and worry about the dissension and the wickedness his son was causing among those who were within the Church. (See Mosiah 27:14.) Our Father in Heaven has also lost many of His spirit children to the world; He knows the feelings of your heart.

Second, we should remember that errors of judgment are generally less serious than errors of intent.

Third, even if there was a mistake made with full knowledge and understanding, there is the principle of repentance for release and comfort. Rather than constantly dwelling on what we perceive as a mistake or a sin or a failure to the detriment of our progress in the gospel or our association with family and friends, it would be better for us to turn away from it. As with any mistake, we may repent by being sorrowful and by attempting to correct or rectify the consequences, to whatever extent possible. We should look forward with renewed faith.

Fourth, don't give up hope for a boy or a girl who has strayed. Many who have appeared to be completely lost have returned. We must be prayerful and, if possible, let our children know of our love and concern.

Fifth, remember that ours was not the only influence

that contributed to the actions of our children, whether those actions were good or bad.

Sixth, know that our Heavenly Father will recognize the love and the sacrifice, the worry and the concern, even though our great effort has been unsuccessful. Parents' hearts are ofttimes broken, yet they must realize that the ultimate responsibility lies with the child after parents have taught correct principles.

Seventh, whatever the sorrow, whatever the concern, whatever the pain and anguish, look for a way to turn it to beneficial use—perhaps in helping others to avoid the same problems, or perhaps by developing a greater insight into the feelings of others who are struggling in a similar way. Surely we will have a deeper understanding of the love of our Heavenly Father when, through prayer, we finally come to know that He understands and wants us to look forward.

The eighth and final point of reminder is that everyone is different. Each of us is unique. Each child is unique. Just as each of us starts at a different point in the race of life, and just as each of us has different strengths and weaknesses and talents, so each child is blessed with his own special set of characteristics. We must not assume that the Lord will judge the success of one in precisely the same way as another. As parents we often assume that if our child doesn't become an overachiever in every way, we have failed. We should be careful in our judgments.

Let us not misunderstand. The responsibilities of parenthood are of the greatest importance. The results of our efforts will have eternal consequences for us and the sons and daughters we raise. Anyone who becomes a parent is under strict obligation to protect and love his children and assist them to return to their Heavenly Father. All parents should understand that the Lord will not hold guiltless those who neglect those responsibilities.

After the Exodus and while Israel was in the wilderness, Moses, in teaching his people, instructed them that the commandments of the Lord should be taught by parents to their children in the home. He said to them:

"And these words, which I command thee this day, shall be in thine heart:

"And thou shalt teach them diligently unto thy children, and shalt talk of them when thou sittest in thine house, and when thou walkest by the way, and when thou liest down, and when thou risest up." (Deuteronomy 6:6–7.)

We should never let Satan fool us into thinking that all is lost. Let us take pride in the good and right things we have done; reject and cast out of our lives those things that are wrong; look to the Lord for forgiveness, strength, and comfort; and then move onward.

A successful parent is one who has loved, one who has sacrificed, and one who has cared for, taught, and ministered to the needs of a child. If you have done all of these and your child is still wayward or troublesome or worldly, it could well be that you are, nevertheless, a successful parent. Perhaps there are children who have come into the world that would challenge any set of parents under any set of circumstances. Likewise, perhaps there are others who would bless the lives of, and be a joy to, almost any father or mother.

I am concerned that there are parents who may be pronouncing harsh judgments upon themselves and may be allowing these feelings to destroy their lives, when in fact they have done their best and should continue in faith. May all who are parents find joy in their efforts with their children.

From an address given at the October 1983 general conference while President Hunter was serving as a member of the Quorum of the Twelve Apostles. (See *Ensign,* Nov. 1983, pp. 63–65.)

Fundamentals of Enduring Family Relationships

PRESIDENT EZRA TAFT BENSON

Marriage is the rock foundation, the cornerstone, of civilization. No nation will ever rise above its homes.

Marriage and family life are ordained of God.

In an eternal sense, salvation is a family affair. God holds parents responsible for their stewardship in rearing their family. It is a most sacred responsibility.

Today we are aware of great problems in our society. The most obvious are sexual promiscuity, homosexuality, drug abuse, alcoholism, vandalism, pornography, and violence. These grave problems are symptoms of failure in the home—the disregarding of principles and practices established by God in the very beginning.

Because parents have departed from the principles the Lord gave for happiness and success, families throughout the world are undergoing great stress and trauma. Many parents have been enticed to abandon their responsibilities in the home to seek after an elusive "self-fulfillment." Some have abdicated parental responsibilities for pursuit of material things, unwilling to postpone personal gratification in the interest of their children's welfare.

It is time to awaken to the fact that there are deliberate efforts to restructure the family along the lines of humanistic values. Images of the family and of love as depicted in television and film often portray a philosophy contrary to the commandments of God.

If one doubts that the family as an institution is being restructured, consider these facts:

Nearly one out of every three marriages ends in divorce.

The traditional family—one which has a husband, a wife not working outside the home, and children—constitutes only 14 percent of American households. (Current Population Reports, 1980.)

Nearly fifty percent of the work force is now female.

About 56 percent of these female workers are mothers with preschool children, and nearly 60 percent of them have teenagers at home.

In the United States alone it is estimated that eight to ten million youngsters, six and under, are in child-care situations outside the home.

Almost one-fifth of all children in the United States live in one-parent homes.

No society will long survive without mothers who care for their young and provide that nurturing care so essential for their normal development.

Innocent-sounding phrases are now used to give approval to sinful practices. Thus, the term "alternative lifestyle" is used to justify adultery and homosexuality, "freedom of choice" to justify abortion, "meaningful relationship" and "self-fulfillment" to justify sex outside of marriage.

If we continue with present trends, we can expect to have more emotionally disturbed young people, more divorce, more depression, and more suicide.

The family is the most effective place to instill lasting values in its members. Where family life is strong and based on principles and practices of the gospel of Jesus Christ, these problems do not as readily appear.

My message this morning is to return to the God-ordained fundamentals that will ensure love, stability, and happiness in our homes. May I offer three fundamentals to happy, enduring family relationships.

First: *A husband and wife must attain righteous unity and oneness in their goals, desires, and actions.*

Marriage itself must be regarded as a sacred covenant before God. A married couple have an obligation not only to each other but to God. He has promised blessings to those who honor that covenant.

Fidelity to one's marriage vows is absolutely essential for love, trust, and peace. Adultery is unequivocally condemned by the Lord.

Husbands and wives who love each other will find that love and loyalty are reciprocated. This love will provide a nurturing atmosphere for the emotional growth of children. Family life should be a time of happiness and joy that children can look back on with fond memories and associations.

Hear these simple admonitions from the Lord which may be applied to the marriage covenant.

First: "See that ye love one another; cease to be covetous; learn to impart one to another as the gospel requires. . . . Cease to be unclean; cease to find fault one with another." (D&C 88:123–24.)

Second: "Thou shalt love thy wife with all thy heart, and shalt cleave unto her and none else. . . . Thou shalt not commit adultery." (D&C 42:22, 24.)

Third: "He that hath the spirit of contention is not of me, but is of the devil, who is the father of contention." (3 Nephi 11:29.)

And there are many more scriptural admonitions.

Restraint and self-control must be ruling principles in the marriage relationship. Couples must learn to bridle their tongues as well as their passions.

Prayer in the home and prayer with each other will strengthen your union. Gradually thoughts, aspirations, and ideas will merge into a oneness until you are seeking the same purposes and goals.

Rely on the Lord, the teachings of the prophets, and the

scriptures for guidance and help, particularly when there may be disagreements and problems.

Spiritual growth comes by solving problems together—not by running from them. Today's inordinate emphasis on individualism brings egotism and separation. Two individuals becoming "one flesh" is still the Lord's standard. (See Genesis 2:24.)

The secret of a happy marriage is to serve God and each other. The goal of marriage is unity and oneness, as well as self-development. Paradoxically, the more we serve one another, the greater is our spiritual and emotional growth.

The first fundamental, then, is to work toward righteous unity.

Second: *Nurture your children with love and the admonitions of the Lord.*

Rearing happy, peaceful children is no easy challenge in today's world, but it can be done, and it is being done.

Responsible parenthood is the key.

Above all else, children need to know and feel they are loved, wanted, and appreciated. They need to be assured of that often. Obviously, this is a role parents should fill, and most often the mother can do it best.

Children need to know who they are in the eternal sense of their identity. They need to know that they have an eternal Heavenly Father on whom they can rely, to whom they can pray, and from whom they can receive guidance. They need to know from whence they came so that their lives will have meaning and purpose.

Children must be taught to pray, to rely on the Lord for guidance, and to express appreciation for the blessings that are theirs. I recall kneeling at the bedsides of our young children, helping them with their prayers.

Children must be taught right from wrong. They can and must learn the commandments of God. They must be taught that it is wrong to steal, lie, cheat, or covet what others have.

Children must be taught to work at home. They should

learn there that honest labor develops dignity and self-respect. They should learn the pleasure of work, of doing a job well.

The leisure time of children must be constructively directed to wholesome, positive pursuits. Too much time viewing television can be destructive, and pornography in this medium should not be tolerated. It is estimated that growing children today watch television more than twenty-five hours per week.

Communities have a responsibility to assist the family in promoting wholesome entertainment. What a community tolerates will become tomorrow's standard for today's youth.

Families must spend more time together in work and recreation. Family home evenings should be scheduled once a week as a time for recreation, work projects, skits, songs around the piano, games, special refreshments, and family prayers. Like iron links in a chain, this practice will bind a family together, in love, pride, tradition, strength, and loyalty.

Family study of the scriptures should be the practice in our homes each Sabbath day.

Daily devotionals are also a commendable practice, where scripture reading, singing of hymns, and family prayer are a part of our daily routine.

Third: *Parents must prepare their children for the ordinances of the gospel.*

The most important teachings in the home are spiritual. Parents are commanded to prepare their sons and daughters for the ordinances of the gospel: baptism, confirmation, priesthood ordinations, and temple marriage. They are to teach them to respect and honor the Sabbath day, to keep it holy. Most important, parents are to instill within their children a desire for eternal life and to earnestly seek that goal above all else.

Eternal life may be obtained only by obedience to the laws and ordinances of the gospel.

When parents themselves have complied with the

ordinances of salvation, when they have set the example of a temple marriage, not only is their own marriage more likely to succeed but their children are far more likely to follow their example.

Parents who provide such a home will have, as the Lord has said, "a house of prayer, a house of fasting, a house of faith, a house of learning, . . . a house of order, a house of God." (D&C 88:119.) Regardless of how modest or humble that home may be, it will have love, happiness, peace, and joy. Children will grow up in righteousness and truth and will desire to serve the Lord.

One past Church President gave this counsel to parents:

"The home is what needs reforming. Try today, and tomorrow, to make a change in your home by praying twice a day with your family. . . . Ask a blessing upon every meal you eat. Spend ten minutes . . . reading a chapter from the words of the Lord in the [scriptures]. . . . Let love, peace, and the Spirit of the Lord, kindness, charity, sacrifice for others, abound in your families. Banish harsh words, . . . and let the Spirit of God take possession of your hearts. Teach to your children these things, in spirit and power. . . . Not one child in a hundred would go astray, if the home environment, example and training, were in harmony with . . . the gospel of Christ." (Joseph F. Smith, *Gospel Doctrine*, 5th ed. [Salt Lake City: Deseret Book Co., 1939], p. 302.)

I testify that by following these precepts and practices, serious problems with the family can and will be avoided.

Thank God for the joys of family life. I have often said there can be no genuine happiness separate and apart from a good home. The sweetest influences and associations of life are there. God bless us to strengthen our homes with love and unity and by following His precepts.

From an address given at the October 1982 general conference while President Benson was serving as President of the Quorum of the Twelve Apostles. (See *Ensign*, Nov. 1982, pp. 59–61.)

Home First

ELDER REX D. PINEGAR

Some time ago in a neighborhood not far from my home, dozens of bright, yellow balloons were seen floating from every tree branch and light post lining a winding, three-block road. It was a beautiful sight on that hazy winter day. Senses were stirred as one drove with anticipation along that friendly, colorful street. Around each bend in the road rose the yellow balloons, waving upward to the top of the hill where they warmly proclaimed: WELCOME HOME, BRIGHAM! I had heard of Brigham Fordham only a few months earlier when I was told of the tragic accident that left him paralyzed. He was only eighteen years old. I now discovered that this was his home and his homecoming from the hospital.

I noticed the ramp that had been built onto the front of the house and thought of other changes that would have been made in his home to accommodate the changes in his life. There will be changes in Brigham's family, too, I thought. Life will be different for all the Fordhams—and, perhaps, difficult.

But as the yellow balloons brightly signaled to Brigham and to all who had the opportunity to travel this street, his was a caring home where family love and strength would be found.

Our Heavenly Father has organized us into families for the purpose of helping us successfully meet the trials and challenges of life. The home also exists to bless us with the joys and privileges of family associations. Our family is our safety place, our support network, our sanctuary, and our salvation.

Our homes should be "the strong place to which children can come for the anchor they need in this day of trouble and turmoil," said President Harold B. Lee. (*His Servants Speak*, comp. R. Clayton Brough [Bountiful, Utah: Horizon, 1975], p. 154.)

In his book *The Power of the Family*, Dr. Paul Pearsall declares there is a "power of loving energy that flows within every family circle during the joy of the best of times and particularly at times of the sorrow of the worst of times." (New York: Doubleday, 1990, p. 354.)

He states, "No matter what the form of your family, from single-parent household to the largest multi-generation family in your town, your work at keeping families together is the job of saving our world." (Ibid., p. 351.)

The Lord, through His prophets, has taught us of the divine power and influence of the home.

"There is no substitute for the home," said President Joseph F. Smith. "Its foundation is as ancient as the world, and its mission has been ordained of God from the earliest times. . . .

"There can be no genuine happiness separate and apart from the home, and every effort made to sanctify and pre-serve its influence is uplifting to those who toil and sacrifice for its establishment. There is no happiness without service and there is no greater service than that which converts the home into a divine institution, and which promotes and preserves family life." (*Gospel Doctrine*, 5th ed. [Salt Lake City: Deseret Book Co., 1939], p. 300.)

On the night of September 21, 1989, Hurricane Hugo passed with all its fury over the beautiful city of Charleston, South Carolina. My good friend Alvie Evans lived in a low-lying area near the water, where the maximum strength of the storm was headed. He gathered his family together and moved to higher ground, to the home of his mother.

Late in the night, 150-mile-per-hour winds raged around them, uprooting trees and ripping away parts of the house. The storm became so severe that the Evans family feared they would experience physical harm. Alvie, with his wife and children, his mother and his brothers and sister and their families, knelt together in the entrance hall of the home and prayed humbly to the Lord, asking for protection and for safety.

The next morning they viewed the devastation. Of the fifty or more large, strong oak trees that had been growing in his mother's yard, only eight remained standing. There was damage to the house, the cars, the entire city, but the family was safe. The Lord had heard their prayers and had protected them through the storm. Alvie said, "I didn't know then if we would have a house to return to, but I knew we would always have a home, because our family was intact and secure."

President David O. McKay once said, "There is nothing temporary in the home of the Latter-day Saint." (In *Conference Report*, June 1919, p. 77.)

He also stated: "[One] can have a beautiful house with all the decorations that modern art can give or wealth bestow. [It can] have all the outward forms that will please the eye and yet not [be] a home. . . . It may be a hovel, a log hut, a tent, a wickiup, if you have the right spirit within, the true love of Christ, and love for one another—fathers and mothers for the children, children for parents, husband and wife for each other—you have the true life of the home that Latter-day Saints build and which they are striving to establish." (*Gospel Ideals* [Salt Lake City: Improvement Era, 1953], pp. 480–81.)

Today, evil forces are challenging the home as never before. If our homes are to endure, parents and children must dedicate themselves to the gospel ideals that ensure preservation of home and family.

Dr. Pearsall expresses the opinion that families aren't

failing but we are failing the family because we have not learned how to put family life first in our world. "Our society is interfering with the family-first feature," he writes. "We are in familial bankruptcy and have fallen into the hands of receivers such as schools, businesses, recreational pursuits, and numerous institutional demands. The issue is not one of setting priorities; the issue is one of making difficult choices for the family. There can only be one number one," he stresses. "Is it your family?" He makes this emphatic statement: "I warn you that if your family does not come first, your family will not last." (*Power of the Home*, p. 18.)

In homes where high ideals and gospel values are maintained, it is parents, not teachers, who lay the foundation of character and faith in the hearts of their children. If the training a child should receive in the home is neglected, neither the Church nor the school can compensate for the loss.

In recent instruction from the First Presidency and the Twelve, President Thomas S. Monson pointed out that "the primary responsibility for building testimonies and providing faith-building experiences in our members, including our youth, resides in the home. The Church should continue to support the determination of the family to do this." President Monson encouraged priesthood leaders to "increase their efforts to build strong, gospel-centered homes." (*Ensign*, May 1990, p. 92.)

The Church functions to make it possible for its members to live the gospel more fully in their homes. To assist us in this vital endeavor, major changes in Church budgeting policies have been made which Elder Boyd K. Packer said "will have the effect of returning much of the responsibility for teaching and counseling and activity to the family where it belongs. . . . There will be fewer intrusions into family schedules and in the family purses.

"Church activities must be replaced by family activities."

Elder Packer closed his instruction by saying, "It is a course correction; it is an inspired move." (*Ensign,* May 1990, p. 89.)

Only when parents and children work together for the same high objective—to put home and family first—can the home be preserved as God intended.

Some time ago we had a special opportunity for a family get-together. A married daughter and her husband came with their three little boys for a short stay before their move from the East Coast of the United States to the West Coast. Another married daughter and her husband came with their four children from out of town to make it possible for the entire family to be together for a weekend.

On Sunday evening all of our family gathered in our home just to celebrate being together—"all under one roof again," exclaimed my wife. She had planned a special program for the occasion, with the appropriate theme, "Making Memories." She had a recording of one of our daughters singing a song about memories. She had obtained copies of a particular book about the subject as a special gift for each son and daughter. To make the memory of that weekend really complete, there would be a family picture taken. Every detail about the evening had been meticulously planned. It would be certain to create a happy memory for each family member. Or would it?

While the beautiful song played softly in the background, the living room filled with the noise and laughter of our growing family circle. The grandchildren couldn't sit still. They giggled and teased and played happily with one another. The grownup children enjoyed each other, too, and all talked at once, it seemed, about days gone by and about the future. They laughed with each other and laughed at the antics of their children, who by now were having tickling matches on the floor or sticking little fingers into the chocolate mint cake. It had become frustrating—and funny!

I don't know which was more frustrating or funny—the

family program which ended soon after it began, with Bonnie, the would-be "memory-maker," sighing, "Oh, what's the use? No one's listening!" or the photo session, with twelve frenzied adults all trying unsuccessfully to pose eleven overactive, squirming children. Was this a family celebration? Or was it a family circus? One thing I knew, this was not the way Bonnie had intended it to be. She had wanted this time of family gathering to be meaningful and memorable.

A few days after everyone had gone and our house was again very quiet, a little book came for us. It was a picture book about families, and it was inscribed: "To my warm and loving, full-of-fun family—every one of you," with a special note added for Mom: "Here's to the wonderful chaos, the wonderful photos, the wonderful gathering place, the wonderful memories you so lovingly help to create each time we're together."

Later, this note from another daughter: "Thank you for a wonderful stay. The boys haven't been this happy in many months. It has been so nice for them to feel so loved and to have a little extra attention and spoiling. I'm so glad we could all watch together as Clark learned to walk, and that he could start forming his special bonds with loving grandparents, aunts, uncles, and cousins. Our children couldn't be more blessed to have such a loving, supportive family network."

A son stated that being home with the family was always a happy time.

Another daughter wrote this:

> If you could see my house of dreams,
> No palace would it be
> But just where I feel happiest—
> You are that home to me.

Within that "wonderful chaos" of our family, all is obviously not perfect. There are problems in our family, as in many families—challenges related to serious illness, aging parents, schooling, employment, and others. However, individual burdens and concerns may be lightened by the power of a family united in mutual love and support and in prayers of faith.

Following the well-known statement "No other success can compensate for failure in the home," President David O. McKay went on to say: "The poorest shack in which love prevails over a united family is of greater value to God and future humanity than any other riches. In such a home God can work miracles and will work miracles." (In Conference Report, Apr. 1964, p. 5.)

On a Sunday morning a few years ago, Donald Pinnell, now president of the Amarillo Texas Stake, was attending church in his branch in Tucumcari, when suddenly someone brought him the alarming news, "Brother Pinnell, your home is on fire!"

President Pinnell quickly found his two sons, ages twelve and sixteen, and headed toward his ranch. His first thoughts were of his wife, who had stayed home that day recuperating from recent surgery. He had no word about her until the driver of a returning fire truck stopped along the way to tell him she was safe.

Brother and Sister Pinnell had just built their dream home, a Spanish-style house on their ranch fifty miles out in the country. It was a very nice home and a source of great pleasure to their family.

As he and his boys approached the top of the terrain, they could see in the distance the smoke coming from their burning home. Donald Pinnell said of that moment, "We could tell that our home was completely engulfed in flames; and I just stopped the car at the top of the hill for a few minutes. I said to my sons, 'Now look, you can spend all your life storing up treasures of the earth, and you can sit on a hill and watch them go up in flames, or, you can store up the right kind of treasures and take them with you through eternity.'"

The right kind of treasures are our families and those divine attributes and qualities of character that are taught and learned in gospel-centered homes. May we make the necessary individual and family course corrections which will put the Lord and our families first and fill our homes with these eternal treasures.

From an address given at the April 1990 general conference while Elder Pinegar was serving in the Presidency of the Seventy. (See *Ensign,* May 1990, pp. 9–11.)

We Are Family

PRESIDENT ELAINE L. JACK

Several years ago a baseball team from the East won the World Series. They hit as well as any club, they fielded the ball with skill and precision, but what really set them apart was their constant reference to a simple phrase in a popular song: "We are family." They were a unit. Diverse in age, style, size, training, and circumstance, yes, but "We are family" was their magic.

In every home let it be said, "We are family."

I believe in families. I believe that families are central to the Father's plan; families are the basic foundation of the kingdom of God on earth. It is in the family that we teach principles of righteousness. It is to our families that we turn for comfort and congratulations. Families bring us our deepest challenges and our greatest joys.

When I was set apart as general president of the Relief Society, President Thomas S. Monson said, "This is a time of great change in the world and in the church as we observe modifications in family style and family characteristics. We recognize that there are many single-parent families; there are families where difficulties exist. . . . Furthermore, we find encroachment of the drug culture and other challenges which cause stress in families. You at this hour have been called . . . to direct the organization that can provide that ameliorating influence, that balm of Gilead." I have taken that blessing to heart.

Often when I talk about the family, I am not referring to some picture-perfect family—father, mother, children, cat, dog, and maybe two goldfish. That image is so hard to replicate. And yet, from so many families comes the cry, "I don't fit in."

Nothing could be further from the truth. When I say *family*, I think of those I love the most, those I long to be near when they are gone, and those whose opinions I value, whose needs are my needs, whose problems are my problems. That picture of a family has very little to do with numbers or circumstance and everything to do with the commandment, "Love one another."

I think of a woman in Massachusetts who wrote me shortly after I was called as general Relief Society president. She lamented that she didn't feel she "fit in" with Relief Society because most of her life had been oriented toward raising her sons and "practicing soccer, or wrestling, exploring muddy caves, building bonfires, and helping to design better paper airplanes." I understood. I have a family of all boys as well.

I think of my husband's partner who lost his wife a year ago. In the family Christmas letter he wrote, "We have gotten through this first year remarkably well. We feel her influence all the time and that has helped."

I think of a dear friend who was raised by a single mother. This young woman, now raising a family of her own, sings the praises of what she calls "the model mother who doubled as a father as well."

Are there families who fit and families who don't? I don't think so. The family is an organization with many variables and many struggles. An Oriental proverb says, "No one can say of his house: There is no trouble here."

In particular, I want to address single parents. They are raising children; they are helping with grandchildren—in fact, some are raising grandchildren. They are stalwart aunts and uncles. They are neighbors and friends.

Single parents face circumstances that are different from those of traditional homes. Still, they share with all parents the need for teaching righteous principles in an increasingly unrighteous world. It is gospel principles that hold us steady amid crisis and change. Gospel principles drive our decisions. These principles allow us to stand firm, to listen to the Spirit rather than drift with the wind of popular opinion.

President Ezra Taft Benson has said: "The family is the most effective place to instill lasting values in its members. Where family life is strong and based on principles and practices of the gospel of Jesus Christ, . . . problems do not as readily appear." (*Ensign,* Nov. 1982, p. 59.)

Some of the principles that are crucial for Latter-day Saint families today are obedience, trust, respect, forgiveness, order and patience, charity and love. Indeed, a good motto for families is the thirteenth article of faith: "We believe in being honest, true, chaste, benevolent, virtuous, and in doing good to all men; indeed, we may say that we follow the admonition of Paul—We believe all things, we hope all things, we have endured many things, and hope to be able to endure all things. If there is anything virtuous, lovely, or of good report or praiseworthy, we seek after these things."

This isn't a wish list; it is a work list. Those are principles. They are crucial. As the storm closes in on us, we can no longer be casual in our beliefs. We must be passionate about our beliefs; that passion for gospel principles must be taught in our homes. With those principles in place, or at least in process, families are prepared to face the world, for the Lord has promised, "If ye are prepared ye shall not fear." (D&C 38:21.)

Today there is a growing concern for families. The press and pollsters continually report that the family is in trouble. They speak of families disintegrating, families hungry and homeless, families in flux, and family violence. No wonder! The adversary is stepping up his efforts to disrupt the influence and focus of good families. Satan is orchestrating the demise of the family.

Satan is seeing success in his crusade to set aside the sacred calling of motherhood. He is now turning his forces on the whole family. President Spencer W. Kimball prophesied: "The time will come when only those who believe deeply and actively in the family will be able to preserve their families in the midst of the gathering evil around us." (*Ensign*, Nov. 1980, p. 4.)

All homes confront challenges. Single parents in particular can testify to the trials of keeping it all together. One mother wrote, "I work 45 to 50 hours every week and pray like the dickens my child support will come in the mail."

Holding fast to our principles can help reverse the evil gathering momentum around us. It won't be easy, but it will be worth it. Three things can make a significant difference: First, draw upon the powers of heaven to help you. Second, maintain balance in your own life. And third, make memories that will last a lifetime.

When the Lord said, "Be not weary in well doing," I think He was talking to parents, many of them single. He knows directing a family requires hard work and is often exhausting. Our greatest resource is the Lord and the powers of heaven. Prayer, therefore, is a powerful beginning to resolving or coping with difficulties of this life. When you need someone, talk to the Lord. So many times I have turned to Him, sometimes on my knees and sometimes in my heart in the middle of a crisis in a very busy room. He has responded with answers, or peace of mind, a resolve simply to go on, or even an angel of mercy in the shape of a neighbor or friend.

As we pray, we teach of a loving father who is near. In our home, we tried always to have evening family prayers. As we gathered together, our teenaged son David, when it was his turn to pray, would often look around and say, "Anyone need anything"? He had learned the principle to go to the Lord in prayer and to ask for help.

Draw upon the strength in the scriptures. The accounts

in the scriptures are more than just good stories; they are examples of the Lord building good people, one experience at a time. So it is with us. We learn of hardship from Alma, of commitment from Ruth, of trials from Job, of humility from Moses, of repentance from Peter. We learn from Him whose world this is when we read the scriptures.

A sister in Colombia came into the Church, a young, twenty-three-year-old widow, and she expected her life to change immediately for the better. She said, "I would ask how this could be the true church if God didn't provide any miracles for those that entered it, to solve their problems." She took the advice of one of her Church leaders who said, "Read the scriptures and there you will find that our Heavenly Father loves you . . . you're a daughter of God. Diligently keep His commandments, and He'll do His part for you." She now recounts, "Today the storms are still there, my two small children have become lovely companions, loving and understanding, and I can see that I wasn't the one who sought to push them forward. My Heavenly Father was always at my side . . . faithful and sincere."

Seek the blessings of the priesthood. If priesthood power can bring manna from heaven, it can bring personal revelation as well. A sister in Chile has shared a blessed family experience: "I was impressed with how the elder, all dressed in white, lifted his arm to the square and said the prayer and baptized my mother. I will never forget that moment. . . . It was as if I was remembering something from another lifetime."

Second, balance your life. Once you've got a plan for your spiritual needs, take a long look at your temporal burdens. This is particularly important when as a single parent you carry all the load. The first thing to do is reposition the weight. It's like having your tires balanced so that the car rides smoothly on all four wheels, no one tire taking all the bumps. And dump what you don't need.

Part of your balancing act is to let others help you.

Single parents may feel that acting self-sufficient, capable, able to leap tall buildings in a single bound, gives the impression that everything is just fine. Such an approach may be commendable at times, for a while it may salve the pain of rejection or loss, but it will eventually make the going more difficult.

A good friend of mine, now a widow, told me how she learned about balance before her husband died. She was busy getting things done at home, and the more she worked, the more she fumed that her husband wasn't helping her. He was just going about his business. Finally, sensing her frustration, he said to her, "Just tell me when you need me and what you want me to do. I can't read your mind." Then he added, "You're a hard person to help."

I think many of us are. We all need packhorses to help carry the load. They can be home teachers, visiting teachers, neighbors, brothers, sisters, or even children. Some of my best advice comes from my son Bill who, though thousands of miles away, calls to talk about my ideas or talks I have to give. He is wise, and I willingly take his counsel.

I know of a doctor's assistant who each Sunday morning before church services goes to the home of her boss, not far from her home, to help his little girls curl their hair. A widower, this surgeon is awfully good with a scalpel and stitches, but he can't do anything with long hair. The assistant knows that little things make a big difference.

Balance is maintained by taking some time for ourselves. I go on long walks to fill up my soul. Being out in nature stretches my sights beyond the problems of everyday living to the joy of living in this beautiful world. The Australian naturalist Karl Baker said, "I have grown taller from walking with the trees." I understand that feeling. I regain my balance when I look at the world God created, not as a backdrop but as a part of our existence.

Sometimes we have to balance the good and the bad. Hardship is part of this life. People make mistakes; they hurt our feelings; sometimes they injure our very souls. A natural reaction may be to silently scream, "Why me?" But remember the cry of the Savior on the cross, "Father, forgive them; for they know not what they do." (Luke 23:34.) Can we ever reach that measure of Christlike love? As long as bitterness, rejection, hatred, or grief dominate our feelings, our ability to face other challenges is diminished. Forgiveness is the key. It is powerful spiritual medicine. One of the greatest blessings you can give your family is the ability to forgive and move on.

Balance comes from accountability, for with each choice is a consequence. That applies not just to rules but to the principles behind the rules. Why don't we swim on Sunday? Why do we shun violent or sex-laden films? Why do we reach out to those who need assistance? Why do our young men and women choose to serve a mission and embrace the standards of preparation for such a call? Because of our moral values. These values are timeless, and they require us to be discriminating in our choices. Being accountable is being mature about our choices, recognizing the great blessings that come to us for choosing the Lord's way.

And last, make memories that you will want to remember. What is remarkable is that good memories can come from the best of times and the worst of times. For single parents, making the transition from a two-parent home to a one, may mean a series of very bad days, weeks, and months. Rather than hanging on the problems of the past, start immediately making new memories. Go on outings with the family. Go to the park or the mountains. Talk about sunsets and clouds and why we are here, how we all fit together. Play board games, bake cookies but eat some of the dough first, wash the car or the dog or the windows. But do it together.

Some of the best times at my house were at the end of the day when our boys would pile on the bed and begin to talk. They talked openly about what was happening at school and with friends. Now, with them gone, I treasure those late nights. Being focused on family time establishes traditions, gives children a sense that "All is well." They need that security, and so do you.

Many memories are made when you are busy doing other things. An institute teacher told of mowing lawns each summer with his boys. They built up quite a business cutting grass. But this father was quick to point out, "I'm not trying to build a landscape business; I'm trying to build boys into men." They enjoyed the drive between houses when they could talk; they liked surveying what they had done; they helped each other finish tasks; they learned to work together. They could have hung a banner from their makeshift trailer advertising their work—"We are family."

Teaching and applying righteous principles is our challenge today. The Lord has said, "Walk with me." (Moses 6:34.) No one has to walk this life alone. He recognized that at times the wind would be squarely in the face, that often the steps would be solitary and tired, and that the road ahead would seem so very long, no end in sight. A widow in Utah wrote me of just that experience and how she resolved it: "My heartache as a woman alone goes on, but what valuable resources are available to draw on: memories, a deep testimony, past experiences in the gospel, love of family, dear friends, and a great love of my Savior and Redeemer."

Jesus Christ, the Savior of us all, knows what it is like to carry burdens alone. Our burdens are His as well. He is with us, always, for "we are family" and "families are forever."

From addresses given at multistake leadership meetings while President Jack was serving as Relief Society General President.

The Women of God

ELDER NEAL A. MAXWELL

We know so little about the reasons for the division of duties between womanhood and manhood as well as between motherhood and priesthood. These were divinely determined in another time and another place. We are accustomed to focusing on the men of God because theirs is the priesthood and leadership line. But paralleling that authority line is a stream of righteous influence reflecting the remarkable women of God who have existed in all ages and dispensations, including our own. Greatness is not measured by coverage in column inches, either in newspapers or in the scriptures. The story of the women of God, therefore, is, for now, an untold drama within a drama.

We men know the women of God as wives, mothers, sisters, daughters, associates, and friends. You seem to tame us and to gentle us, and, yes, to teach us and to inspire us. For you, we have admiration as well as affection, because righteousness is not a matter of role, nor goodness a matter of gender. In the work of the Kingdom, men and women are not without each other, but do not envy each other, lest by reversals and renunciations of role we make a wasteland of both womanhood and manhood.

Just as certain men were foreordained from before the foundations of the world, so were certain women appointed to certain tasks. Divine design—not chance—brought Mary forward to be the mother of Jesus. The boy prophet Joseph Smith was blessed not only with a great father but also with a superb mother, Lucy Mack, who influenced a whole dispensation.

When we would measure loving loyalty in a human relationship, do we not speak of Ruth and Naomi even more than David and Jonathan? And no wonder God with His perfect regard for women is so insistent about our obligations to widows.

A widow with her mite taught us how to tithe. An impoverished and starving widow with her hungry son taught us how to share, as she gave her meal and oil to Elijah. The divine maternal instincts of an Egyptian woman retrieved Moses from the bulrushes, thereby shaping history and demonstrating how a baby is a blessing—not a burden.

What greater conversation of anticipation has there been than that of Elisabeth and Mary when also the babe in Elisabeth leaped in recognition of Mary? (Luke 1:41.)

Does it not tell us much about the intrinsic intelligence of women to read of the crucifixion scene at Calvary, "And many women were there beholding afar off." (Matthew 27:55.) Their presence was a prayer; their lingering was like a litany.

And who came first to the empty tomb of the risen Christ? Two women.

Who was the first mortal to see the resurrected Savior? Mary of Magdala. Special spiritual sensitivity keeps the women of God hoping long after many others have ceased.

The charity of good women is such that their "love makes no parade"; they are not glad "when others go wrong"; they are too busy serving to sit statusfully about, waiting to be offended. Like Mary, they ponder trustingly those puzzlements that disable others. God trusts women so much that He lets them bear and care for His spirit children.

In our modern kingdom, it is no accident that women were, through the Relief Society, assigned compassionate service. So often the service of women seems instinctive, while that of some men seems more labored. It is precisely because the daughters of Zion are so uncommon that the adversary will not leave them alone.

We salute you, sisters, for the joy that is yours as you rejoice in a baby's first smile and as you listen with eager ear to a child's first day at school, which bespeaks a special selflessness. Women, more quickly than others, will understand the possible dangers when the word *self* is militantly placed before other words like *fulfillment.* You rock a sobbing child without wondering if today's world is passing you by, because you know you hold tomorrow tightly in your arms.

So often our sisters comfort others when their own needs are greater than those being comforted. That quality is like the generosity of Jesus on the cross. Empathy during agony is a portion of divinity!

I thank the Father that His Only Begotten Son did not say in defiant protest at Calvary, "My body is my own!" I stand in admiration of women today who resist the fashion of abortion, by refusing to make the sacred womb a tomb!

When the real history of mankind is fully disclosed, will it feature the echoes of gunfire or the shaping sound of lullabies? The great armistices made by military men or the peacemaking of women in homes and in neighborhoods? Will what happened in cradles and kitchens prove to be more controlling than what happened in congresses? When the surf of the centuries has made the great pyramids so much sand, the everlasting family will still be standing, because it is a celestial institution, formed outside telestial time. The women of God know this.

No wonder the men of God support and sustain you sisters in your unique roles, for the act of deserting home in order to shape society is like thoughtlessly removing crucial fingers from an imperiled dike in order to teach people to swim.

We men love you women for meeting inconsiderateness with consideration and selfishness with selflessness. We are touched by the eloquence of your example. We are deeply grateful for your enduring us as men when we are not at our best because—like God—you love us not only for what we are but for what we have the power to become.

We have special admiration for the unsung but unsullied single women among whom are some of the noblest daughters of God. These sisters know that God loves them, individually and distinctly. They make wise career choices even though they cannot now have the most choice career. Though in their second estate they do not have their first desire, they still overcome the world. These sisters who cannot now enrich the institution of their own marriage so often enrich other institutions in society. They do not withhold their blessings simply because some blessings are now withheld from them. Their trust in God is like that of the wives who are childless, but not by choice, who in the justice of God will receive special blessings one day.

I, along with my brethren of the priesthood, express undying gratitude to our eternal partners. We know that we can go no place that matters without them, nor would we have it otherwise. When we kneel to pray, we kneel together. When we kneel at the altar of the holy temple, we kneel together. When we approach the final gate where Jesus Himself is the gatekeeper, we will, if faithful, pass through that gate together.

The prophet who sits with us today, our beloved President Spencer W. Kimball, could tell us of such togetherness, when at the time of his overwhelming apostolic calling he was consoled by his Camilla, who met his anguished, sobbing sense of inadequacy and, running her fingers through his hair, said, "You can do it, you can do it." He surely has done it, but with her at his side.

Notice, brethren, how all the prophets treat their wives and honor women, and let us do likewise!

Finally, remember: When we return to our real home, it will be with the "mutual approbation" of those who reign in the "royal courts on high." There we will find beauty such as mortal "eye hath not seen"; we will hear sounds of surpassing music which mortal "ear hath not heard." Could such a regal homecoming be possible without the anticipatory arrangements of a Heavenly Mother?

Meanwhile, there are no separate paths back to that heavenly home. Just one straight and narrow way, at the end of which, though we arrive trailing tears, we shall at once be "drenched in joy."

From an address given at the April 1978 general conference while Elder Maxwell was serving in the Presidency of the Seventy. (See *Ensign*, May 1978, pp. 10–11.)

Brethren, Love Your Wives

ELDER JAMES E. FAUST

What should a wife mean to her husband? And how does she deserve to be treated?

No man can become completely adequate or function responsibly without help from others. Of course too much help or the wrong kind of help stifles and is counterproductive. But at the heart of human adequacy is self-esteem, which is fed by rich, life-giving love, confidence, and caring of others. This support can come richly from family and friends. But for men it comes mostly from their wives.

Consequently, there is no higher commitment for any man than to be loyal to his commitment to his God and faith, to his wife and family. The reciprocating fruits from keeping that commitment will usually give him boundless sustaining love and the challenge to reach deep down inside himself and call forth the seeds of the finest of his gifts for their full flowering. He will enjoy a place of honor, dignity, and respect.

Most men worry about succeeding in their life's work and spend much time and effort at their profession. But I've learned that the way to put one's *professional* life in order is to put one's *personal* life in order. How can we be adequate at anything professionally without being adequate as men, husbands, and fathers first? And yet, we often shortchange those who mean most to us, thinking that because of our special training and special knowledge, others have a greater claim on our time and concern than our own families. I fully recognize that the work my wife did in my home was more important to me than any work I did.

The relationship between husband and wife is the linchpin in the whole family relationship. I am sorry that I have come so late to a fuller appreciation of the extent of the needs of our wives and womenfolk for love, appreciation, companionship, and recognition. These needs are great, they are constant, and they need to be frequently met. Kindness and courtesy do not begin in the professional office—they begin at home.

I am also sorry that I have not sooner appreciated the great, sublime, unique gifts which our wives inherit from divinity. I speak of their womanly intuitions and their steadfast faith and capacity to love. Properly nurtured, the eternal relationship of a husband and wife flowers into a love of consummate beauty.

It is an unrighteous exercise of priesthood authority for a man, as a conduit through his priesthood office, to withhold or limit blessings which should flow through the priesthood to his wife and family. The priesthood blessings are not just male- or husband-limited but reach their potential flowering in the eternal relationship of the husband and the wife sharing and administering these great blessings to the family. Our wives have priesthood blessings, though not priesthood offices. These blessings are the keys to eternal life, salvation, and exaltation through obedience.

Elder Boyd K. Packer recently asked me a very penetrating question: "What would you have been without your wife, Ruth?" I could have answered immediately, "Not much," but he already knew that. I took him seriously and spent the next twenty-four hours thinking about what I would have been without the loving, sweet support and the discipline of Ruth Wright in my life. It shocked me a little to even think about what life would be and would have been without her. I would have to answer honestly that without my wife I would have been pretty much of a failure. I do not claim to be an expert in marriage: I have been married only once. But, thanks to my good wife, it took. I do not claim to have a better marriage than anyone, but I do claim to be married to a great companion.

I am still moved by what President Marion G. Romney said to the Twelve in a meeting in the temple a few days after the death of his wife, Sister Ida Romney, which with his permission I share. Said President Romney, "When Ida died, something went out of me. The holding force was gone." At the graveside, President Romney said to me, "Be good to your wife. Take her with you everywhere you can. The time will come when you will not be able to be together."

The most sacred, intimate, and blessed relationship of life is between husband and wife. I do not love anybody like I love my wife. My mother has my father, and my children have their companions, but Ruth is me. Our wives become part of us, and they become like our own flesh— and as Paul counseled, we should love them as such. (See Ephesians 5:28–33.) The simple truth is that it is not good for man to be alone. The greatest sustaining influence in my mature life has been the constant supporting, unqualified, unreserved love I have felt for my wife. The sacred relationship with my wife has been the supreme benediction of my life. I just can't imagine what my life would have been like without having had that blessing.

Without our wives we would never be privileged to be fathers and grandfathers and enjoy all the blessings that that entails. This relation has to come first in all of our relationships with other people. It is the glue that brings together all of the parts of the jigsaw puzzle of eternal joy and fulfillment and happiness.

One of the greatest blessings of having a good wife is that she can be the source of the most basic of all human needs—love. The greatest unreserved love that I have received in my life has been from the good women in my family: my wife, my mother, my mother-in-law, my grand-mothers, my daughters, and my sweet granddaughters.

The example of how to be a man came from others: my father, my grandfather, my uncles, my older brother Gus, and many Church leaders—bishops, stake presidents, and the General Authorities.

If I hadn't married Ruth, I would not have known her mother, Elizabeth Hamilton Wright. She was one of the twenty-two children of James C. Hamilton, bishop of the Millcreek Ward in Salt Lake City for more than twenty-five years. She went only as far as the third grade. Because she had a special gift for teaching children, she was taken out of school to tend and teach the younger children in the family. It used to break my heart to see her struggle to write a simple note, but she had spiritual maturity, wisdom, insight, and faith like my own mother. She understood things completely by the Holy Spirit. I loved her for her greatness and goodness and because she taught my wife so well. And my wife in turn has taught our children and grandchildren.

One of the areas in which our wives perform a very great service is in their loving discipline of us. In their discipline they keep us closer to what we ought to be in our holy callings. In their discipline they teach us. It is part of the polishing we need to fill in the holes in our character and smooth the rough edges and make us more adequate. Together we are a team—we are one.

President N. Eldon Tanner's daughter Isabelle says about her father, which with his knowledge I share, "When Mother married Daddy he was just a farm boy." But she went on to say that when Sister Tanner would give him a loving suggestion, unlike many men who bridle or argue when their wives tell them something that is good for them, he would simply say, "If you think that's what I should do, I'll do it." Listening to Sister Tanner and listening to the Lord has made a very great man out of President Tanner.

I am grateful to many of the Brethren for their examples of kindness and thoughtfulness and solicitude to their wives. When I was in a stake presidency, Elder S. Dilworth Young came to our stake conference. At that time his wife, Gladys, was an invalid, having suffered from a cruel stroke. She remained that way for years. Brother Young made the extra effort to dress her, feed her, and care for her. In all my life I have not seen a greater example of gentleness, kindness, and solicitude than Brother Young showed to Sister Young. It was an example of perfect love. When I obtained his permission to tell of this, he said, "It was the worst thing in the world that could have happened to Gladys and the best thing for me. It made me decent. I learned what love really should be."

Perhaps in these times of great stress we can become what we ought to be in our relationships with our wives. Perhaps the eternal "every day" causes some of us to be more casual than we ought to be. Of course, we love our wives, but perhaps we take them for granted too much of the time. Perhaps too often we fail to express our appreciation to them in little ways. I know I do. We could certainly show more affection and always look upon our companions with love and respect. We can surely be polite and courteous if we try. We can nourish and cherish them.

The simple fact is that few of us could function nearly as well without the support of our gracious and loving wives. They make our homes the heaven on earth which they are. How can I expect God to honor me and be pleased with my service if I do not honor and cherish my very own companion?

In the scriptures we are told that we should not be unequally yoked together. (See 2 Corinthians 6:14.) I fear that in terms of our total person, our wives maybe do a better job than we do in being Christlike, thoughtful, kind, gracious, and loving. I feel that Ruth deserves a better me. As members of the Church, we all have the responsibility to be instruments to impart righteousness to the world. Unless we impart a full measure of righteousness to our wives and families, we will be blunted instruments to the rest of the world.

We must strive for greater spirituality in our relationships, and especially in our homes. Literally taking the Lord into partnership with us will bring us a full measure of peace, happiness, unity, and contentment. We need these blessings in our lives to be what we ought to be—more adequate vessels for the work which we have been commissioned to do. We have the responsibility to bless the lives of others. If our own lives and spiritual batteries are not full and complete, how can we expect to touch the world and bless others?

I know the gospel is true, and I know a substantial part of that gospel is how I treat my Ruth on an hour-to-hour, day-by-day, ongoing basis. I believe that none of us can come into full possession of all of our powers without an eternal companion. I suggest that the ultimate judgment will come to us in terms of what kind of person we have been, what kind of husband we have been, what kind of father we have been, and what kind of family we have raised. Indeed, the Lord has commanded: "Thou shalt love thy wife with all thy heart, and shalt cleave unto her and none else." (D&C 42:22.) That we may do so, I humbly pray.

From an address given at an Association of Mormon Counselors and Psychotherapists convention, 2 October 1980, while Elder Faust was serving as a member of the Quorum of the Twelve Apostles. (See *Ensign*, July 1981, pp. 34–37.)

Within the Clasp of Your Arms

Elder Jeffrey R. Holland

A recent study conducted by the Church has forcefully confirmed statistically what we have been told again and again from the pulpit. That is, if loving, inspired instruction and example are not provided at home, then our related efforts for success in and around Church programs are severely limited. It is increasingly clear that we must teach the gospel to our families personally and live those teachings in our homes or run the risk of discovering too late that a Primary teacher or priesthood adviser or seminary instructor *could* not do for our children what we *would* not do for them.

May I offer just this much encouragement regarding such a great responsibility? What I cherish in my relationship with my son Matt is that he is, along with his mother and sister and brother, my closest, dearest friend. I would rather be here at this priesthood meeting tonight with my son than with any other male companion in this world. I love to be with him. We talk a lot. We laugh a lot. We play one-on-one basketball; we play tennis and racquetball, though I do refuse to play golf with him (that's a private joke). We discuss problems. I am the president of a small university, and he is the president of a large high school class. We compare notes and offer suggestions and share each other's challenges. I pray for him and have cried with him, and I'm immensely proud of him. We've talked long into the night lying on his water bed, a twentieth-century aberration which I know, as part of the punishment of the last days, will one day burst and wash the Hollands helplessly into the streets of Provo (that's another private joke).

I feel I can talk to Matt about how he is enjoying seminary because I try to talk to him about all of his classes at school. We often imagine together what his mission will be like because he knows how much my mission meant to me. And he asks me about temple marriage because he knows I am absolutely crazy about his mother. He wants his future wife to be like her and for them to have what we have.

Now, even as I speak, I know that there are fathers and sons in this meeting tonight who feel they do not have any portion of what is here described. I know there are fathers who would give virtually their very lives to be close again to a struggling son. I know there are sons in our meeting who wish their dads were at their side, tonight or any night. I have wondered how to speak on this assigned topic without sounding self-righteous on the one hand or offending already tender hearts on the other. In answer to that, I simply say to us all, young and old, Never give up. Keep trying, keep reaching, keep talking, keep praying—but never give up. Above all, never pull away from each other.

May I share a brief but painful moment from my own inadequate efforts as a father?

Early in our married life my young family and I were laboring through graduate school at a university in New England. Sister Holland was the Relief Society president in our ward, and I was serving in our stake presidency. I was going to school full-time and teaching half-time. We had two small children then, with little money and lots of pressures. In fact, our life was about like yours.

One evening I came home from long hours at school, feeling the proverbial weight of the world on my shoulders. Everything seemed to be especially demanding and discouraging and dark. I wondered if the dawn would ever come. Then, as I walked into our small student apartment, there was an unusual silence in the room.

"What's the trouble?" I asked. "Matthew has something he wants to tell you," Pat said. "Matt, what do you have to tell me?" He was quietly playing with his toys in the corner of the room, trying very hard not to hear me. "Matt," I said a little louder, "do you have something to tell me?"

He stopped playing but for a moment didn't look up. Then these two enormous, tear-filled brown eyes turned toward me, and with the pain only a five-year-old can know, he said, "I didn't mind Mommy tonight, and I spoke back to her." With that he burst into tears, and his entire little body shook with grief. A childish indiscretion had been noted, a painful confession had been offered, the growth of a five-year-old was continuing, and loving reconciliation could have been wonderfully under way.

Everything might have been just terrific—except for me. If you can imagine such an idiotic thing, I lost my temper. It wasn't that I lost it with Matt—it was with a hundred and one other things on my mind; but he didn't know that, and I wasn't disciplined enough to admit it. He got the whole load of bricks.

I told him how disappointed I was and how much more I thought I could have expected from him. I sounded like the parental pygmy I was. Then I did what I had never done before in his life—I told him that he was to go straight to bed and that I would not be in to say his prayers with him or to tell him a bedtime story. Muffling his sobs, he obediently went to his bedside, where he knelt—alone—to say his prayers. Then he stained his little pillow with tears his father should have been wiping away.

If you think the silence upon my arrival was heavy, you should have felt it now. My wife did not say a word. She didn't have to. I felt terrible!

Later, as we knelt by our own bed, my feeble prayer for blessings upon my family fell back on my ears with a horrible, hollow ring. I wanted to get up off my knees right then and go to Matt and ask his forgiveness, but he was long since peacefully asleep.

My relief was not so soon coming; but finally I fell asleep and began to dream, which I seldom do. I dreamed Matt and I were packing two cars for a move. For some reason his mother and baby sister were not present. As we finished I turned to him and said, "Okay, Matt, you drive one car and I'll drive the other."

This five-year-old very obediently crawled up on the seat and tried to grasp the massive steering wheel. I walked over to the other car and started the motor. As I began to pull away, I looked to see how my son was doing. He was trying—oh, how he was trying. He tried to reach the pedals, but he couldn't. He was also turning knobs and pushing buttons, trying to start the motor. He could scarcely be seen over the dashboard, but there staring out at me again were those same immense, tear-filled, beautiful brown eyes. As I pulled away, he cried out, "Daddy, don't leave me. I don't know how to do it. I am too little." And I drove away.

A short time later, driving down that desert road in my dream, I suddenly realized in one stark, horrifying moment what I had done. I slammed my car to a stop, threw open the door, and started to run as fast as I could. I left car, keys, belongings, and all—and I ran. The pavement was so hot it burned my feet, and tears blinded my straining effort to see this child somewhere on the horizon. I kept running, praying, pleading to be forgiven and to find my boy safe and secure.

As I rounded a curve nearly ready to drop from physical and emotional exhaustion, I saw the unfamiliar car I had left Matt to drive. It was pulled carefully off to the side of the road, and he was laughing and playing nearby. An older man was with him, playing and responding to his games. Matt saw me and cried out something like, "Hi, Dad. We're having fun." Obviously he had already forgiven and forgotten my terrible transgression against him.

But I dreaded the older man's gaze, which followed my every move. I tried to say "Thank you," but his eyes were filled with sorrow and disappointment. I muttered an awkward apology and the stranger said simply, "You should not have left him alone to do this difficult thing. It would not have been asked of you."

With that, the dream ended, and I shot upright in bed. *My* pillow was now stained, whether with perspiration or tears I do not know. I threw off the covers and ran to the little metal camp cot that was my son's bed. There on my knees and through my tears I cradled him in my arms and spoke to him while he slept. I told him that every dad makes mistakes but that they don't mean to. I told him it wasn't his fault I had had a bad day. I told him that when boys are five or fifteen, dads sometimes forget and think they are fifty. I told him that I wanted him to be a small boy for a long, long time, because all too soon he would grow up and be a man and wouldn't be playing on the floor with his toys when I came home. I told him that I loved him and his mother and his sister more than anything in the world and that whatever challenges we had in life we would face them together. I told him that never again would I withhold my affection or my forgiveness from him, and never, I prayed, would he withhold them from me. I told him I was honored to be his father and that I would try with all my heart to be worthy of such a great responsibility.

Well, I have not proven to be the perfect father I vowed to be that night and a thousand nights before and since. But I still want to be, and I believe this wise counsel from President Joseph F. Smith:

"Brethren, . . . If you will keep your [children] close to your heart, within the clasp of your arms; if you will make them . . . feel that you love them . . . and keep them near to you, they will not go very far from you, and they will not commit any very great sin. But it is when you turn them out of the home, turn them out of your affection . . . that [is what] drives them from you. . . .

" . . . Fathers, if you wish your children to be taught in the principles of the gospel, if you wish them to love the truth and understand it, if you wish them to be obedient to and united with you, love them! and prove . . . that you do love them by your every word and act to[ward] them." (*Gospel Doctrine*, 5th ed. [Salt Lake City: Deseret Book Co., 1966], pp. 282, 316.)

Brethren, we all know fatherhood is not an easy assignment, but it ranks among the most imperative ever given, in time or eternity. We must not pull away from our children. We must keep trying, keep reaching, keep praying, keep listening. We must keep them "within the clasp of our arms." That is what friends are for.

From an address given at the April 1983 general conference while Elder Holland was serving as president of Brigham Young University. (See *Ensign*, May 1983, pp. 36–38.)

Bring Up a Child
in the Way He Should Go

PRESIDENT GORDON B. HINCKLEY

Some time ago there came to my office a man from Las Vegas, Nevada. His wife and married daughter were with him. When we had accomplished the purpose of his visit, the younger woman asked if I would accept something from her thirteen-year-old daughter. She unwrapped a painting of two butterflies around a flowering shrub.

The mother explained that her daughter had been struck by a car in a terrible accident when she was four years of age. Her body was badly broken. She was left paralyzed from the shoulders down, a quadriplegic without the use of arms or legs. She had painted this picture holding a brush between her teeth and moving her head.

As I listened to that story, the painting grew in beauty and value before my eyes. It became more than a portrayal of butterflies. It represented remarkable courage in the face of blinding adversity; tenacious practice in holding and moving the brush; pleading prayers for help; faith—the faith of a child, nurtured by loving parents, that she could create beauty notwithstanding her handicap.

Some might say that this is not a masterpiece. Without knowledge of its origin, that could be the judgment. But what is the test of art? Is it not the inspiration which comes from looking at it?

I will hang this small painting in my study so that during occasional hours of struggle there will come into my mind the picture of a beautiful little girl, robbed of the use of her feet and hands, gripping the handle of a paintbrush in her teeth to create a thing of beauty. Thank you, Krystal, for what you have done for me. I hope the telling of your story will bring a new measure of strength to others who, facing discouragement, have felt they could not go on. I hope that your example will be as a polar star to lead them in the darkness through which they stumble.

When I think of those who carry heavy burdens, my mind goes to our beloved prophet. President Ezra Taft Benson wears the mantle of his sacred office, but his activities are seriously limited. We love him. We honor him. We pray for him. We sustain him. And we go forward.

This church is established on principles that are divine. From the day of its organization, it has been led by prophets, and I solemnly testify that the Lord Jesus Christ, whose church it is and whose name it bears, will never let any man or group of men lead it astray. His is the power to remove them if they should ever be found taking the wrong turn.

We have critics both within the Church and without. Although they are vocal and have access to the media, they are relatively few in number. If we were entirely without criticism, we would be concerned. Our responsibility is not to please the world but, rather, to do the will of the Lord, and from the beginning the divine will so often has been contrary to the ways of the world.

These worldly ways appear to be on a course that should be of concern to every thoughtful man and woman. We in America are saddled with a huge financial deficit in our national budget. This has led to astronomical debt. But there is another deficit which, in its long-term implications, is more serious. It is a moral deficit, a decline in values in the lives of the people, which is sapping the very foundation of our society. It is serious in this land. And it is serious in every other nation of which I know.

Some months ago there appeared in the *Wall Street Journal* what was spoken of as an index of what is happening to our culture: "Since 1960, the U.S. population has increased 41%; the gross domestic product has nearly tripled; and total social spending by all levels of government [has experienced] more than a fivefold increase. . . .

"But during the same . . . period there has been a 560% increase in violent crime; a 419% increase in illegitimate births; a quadrupling in divorce rates; a tripling of the percentage of children living in single-parent homes; more than a 200% increase in the teenage suicide rate." (William J. Bennett, "Quantifying America's Decline," *Wall Street Journal*, 15 Mar. 1993.)

The article concludes with a statement from Alexander Solzhenitsyn: "The West . . . has been undergoing an erosion and [an] obscuring of high moral and ethical ideals. The spiritual axis of life has grown dim."

One need not, of course, read statistics to recognize a moral decay that seems to be going on all about us. It is evident in the easy breakup of marriages, in widespread infidelity, in the growth of youth gangs, in the increased use of drugs and the epidemic spread of AIDS, and in a growing disregard for the lives and property of others. It is seen in the defacement of private and public property with graffiti, which destroys beauty and is an insult to art. It is expressed in the language of the gutter, which is brought into our homes.

The endless sex and violence of network TV, the trash of so many motion pictures, the magnified sensuality found in much of modern literature, the emphasis on sex education, a widespread breakdown of law and order—all are manifestations of this decay.

What is the answer? Is there any way to change the course of the ethical and moral slide we are experiencing? I believe there is.

What is happening is simply an ugly expression of the

declining values of our society. Those who are concerned with the problem advocate more legal regulation, large appropriations for increased police forces, tax increases to build additional jails and prisons. These may be needed to deal with the present problems. They may help in the near term. But they will be only as a bandage too small for the sore. They may help in taking care of the fruits, but they will not get at the roots. In searching for remedies, we speak of a greater work that must be done in our schools. But educators have largely abdicated their responsibility for teaching values. The Church is looked to—this and all other churches. I am grateful for what the Pope recently said in Denver in warning against moral pitfalls. I am pleased to note that the Baptists have begun a campaign for chastity. We as a church are doing much, very much, and I think we are accomplishing much. But it is not enough.

When all is said and done, the primary place in building a value system is in the homes of the people.

I read the other day of a father who pleaded with a judge to lock up his son because he could not control him. I do not doubt that he has tried. But it is now too late. Attitudes have been fixed. Habits have become rigid. If we are to turn this tide, the effort must begin with children when they are young and pliable, when they will listen and learn.

Not long after Sister Hinckley and I were married, we built our first home. We had very little money. I did much of the work myself. It would be called "sweat equity" today. The landscaping was entirely my responsibility. The first of many trees that I planted was a thornless honey locust. Envisioning the day when its filtered shade would assist in cooling the house in the summertime, I put it in a place at the corner where the wind from the canyon to the east blew the hardest. I dug a hole, put in the bare root, put soil around it, poured on water, and largely forgot it. It was only a wisp of a tree, perhaps three-quarters of an inch in diameter. It was so supple that I could bend it with ease in any direction. I paid little attention to it as the years passed.

Then one winter day, when the tree was barren of leaves, I chanced to look out the window at it. I noticed that it was leaning to the west, misshapen and out of balance. I could scarcely believe it. I went out and braced myself against it as if to push it upright. But the trunk was now nearly a foot in diameter. My strength was as nothing against it. I took from my toolshed a block and tackle. Attaching one end to the tree and another to a well-set post, I pulled the rope. The pulleys moved a little, and the trunk of the tree trembled slightly. But that was all. It seemed to say, "You can't straighten me. It's too late. I've grown this way because of your neglect, and I will not bend."

Finally in desperation I took my saw and cut off the great heavy branch on the west side. The saw left an ugly scar, more than eight inches across. I stepped back and surveyed what I had done. I had cut off the major part of the tree, leaving only one branch growing skyward.

More than half a century has passed since I planted that tree. My daughter and her family live in that home now. The other day I looked again at the tree. It is large. Its shape is better. It is a great asset to the home. But how serious was the trauma of its youth and how brutal the treatment I used to straighten it.

When it was first planted, a piece of string would have held it in place against the forces of the wind. I could have and should have supplied that string with ever so little effort. But I did not, and it bent to the forces that came against it.

I have seen a similar thing, many times, in children whose lives I have observed. The parents who brought them into the world seem almost to have abdicated their responsibility. The results have been tragic. A few simple anchors would have given them the strength to withstand the forces that have shaped their lives. Now it appears it is too late.

Every individual in the world is a child of a mother and a father. Neither can ever escape the consequences of their parenthood. Inherent in the very act of creation is responsibility for the child who is created. None can with impunity run from that responsibility.

It is not enough simply to provide food and shelter for the physical being. There is an equal responsibility to provide nourishment and direction to the spirit and the mind and the heart. Wrote Paul to Timothy, "But if any provide not for his own, and specially for those of his own house, he hath denied the faith, and is worse than an infidel." (1 Timothy 5:8.)

I am satisfied that Paul was speaking of more than physical nourishment.

Many years ago, President Stephen L Richards, then a Counselor in the First Presidency, speaking from this pulpit made an eloquent plea to put father back at the head of the family. (See Conference Report, Apr. 1958, p. 94.) I repeat that plea to all fathers. Yours is the basic and inescapable responsibility to stand as head of the family. That does not carry with it any implication of dictatorship or unrighteous dominion. It carries with it a mandate that fathers provide for the needs of their families. Those needs are more than food, clothing, and shelter. Those needs include righteous direction and the teaching, by example as well as precept, of basic principles of honesty, integrity, service, respect for the rights of others, and an understanding that we are accountable for that which we do in this life, not only to one another but also to the God of heaven, who is our Eternal Father.

Let every mother realize that she has no greater blessing than the children which have come to her as a gift from the Almighty; that she has no greater mission than to rear them in light and truth, and understanding and love; that she will have no greater happiness than to see them grow into young men and women who respect principles of virtue, who walk free from the stain of immorality and from the shame of delinquency. Said the writer of Proverbs, "Train up a child in the way he should go: and when he is old, he will not depart from it." (Proverbs 22:6.)

The health of any society, the happiness of its people, their prosperity, and their peace all find their roots in the teaching of children by fathers and mothers. The very structure of our society is now threatened by broken homes and the tragic consequences of those homes.

I believe that with effort we can change this course. We must begin with parents. We must provide understanding on the part of every man and woman of the eternal purposes of life, of the obligations of marriage, and of the responsibilities of parenthood. To men who beget children and then abandon them, I say that God will hold you accountable, for these are also His children, whose cries over what you have done reach up to Him. With the obligation to beget goes the responsibility to nurture, to protect, to teach, to guide in righteousness and truth. Yours is the power and the responsibility to preside in a home where there is peace and security, love and harmony.

I remind mothers everywhere of the sanctity of your calling. No other can adequately take your place. No responsibility is greater, no obligation more binding than that you rear in love and peace and integrity those whom you have brought into the world.

To both of you, let no bickering cloud the spirit of your home. Set aside your selfishness in the interest of a far greater and eternal cause. Bring up your children in light and truth as the Lord has commanded.

Could you wish for anything more than peace for your children? Could you benefit society in any better way? I make you a solemn and sacred promise that if you will do this, the time will come when, looking upon those you have created, nurtured, and loved, you will see the fruits of your nurturing and get on your knees and thank the Lord for His blessing to you.

Now, with all of this, I know there are very many of you who are wonderful parents and whose children are growing in righteousness. Happy and productive will be their lives, and the world will be the better for them. I thank you and most warmly congratulate you. Surely you are fortunate.

But there are others—too many among our own—whose children, to quote the revelation, are "growing up in wickedness" and who "seek not . . . the riches of eternity, but their eyes are full of greediness." (D&C 68:31.) To these I make my appeal.

It may not be easy. It may be fraught with disappointment and challenge. It will require courage and patience. I remind you of the faith and determination of the thirteen-year-old girl who, holding a paintbrush in her teeth, created the painting I showed you earlier. Love can make the difference—love generously given in childhood and reaching through the awkward years of youth. It will do what money lavished on children will never do.

—And patience, with a bridling of the tongue and self-mastery over anger. The writer of Proverbs declared, "A soft answer turneth away wrath." (Proverbs 15:1.)

—And encouragement that is quick to compliment and slow to criticize.

These, with prayers, will accomplish wonders. You cannot expect to do it alone. You need heaven's help in rearing heaven's child—your child, who is also the child of his or her Heavenly Father.

O God, our Eternal Father, bless the parents to teach with love and patience and encouragement those who are most precious, the children who have come from Thee, that together they might be safeguarded and directed for good and, in the process of growth, bring blessings to the world of which they will be a part.

From an address given at the October 1993 general conference while President Hinckley was serving as First Counselor in the First Presidency. (See *Ensign,* Nov. 1993, pp. 54, 59–60.)

Precious Children — a Gift from God

PRESIDENT THOMAS S. MONSON

From the book of Matthew we learn that after Jesus and His disciples descended from the Mount of Transfiguration, they paused at Galilee and then went to Capernaum. The disciples said unto Jesus, "Who is the greatest in the kingdom of heaven?

"And Jesus called a little child unto him, and set him in the midst of them,

"And said, Verily I say unto you, Except ye be converted, and become as little children, ye shall not enter into the kingdom of heaven.

"Whosoever therefore shall humble himself as this little child, the same is greatest in the kingdom of heaven.

"And whoso shall receive one such little child in my name receiveth me.

"But whoso shall offend one of these little ones which believe in me, it were better for him that a millstone were hanged about his neck, and that he were drowned in the depth of the sea." (Matthew 18:1–6.)

I think it significant that Jesus loved these little ones who so recently had left the premortal existence to come to earth. Children then and children now bless our lives, kindle our love, and prompt our good deeds.

Is it any wonder that the poet Wordsworth speaks thus of our birth: "Trailing clouds of glory do we come/From God, who is our home." (William Wordsworth, "Ode: Intimations of Immortality from Recollections of Early Childhood.")

Most of these little ones come to parents who eagerly await their arrival, mothers and fathers who rejoice to be a part of that miracle we call birth. No sacrifice is too great, no pain too severe, no waiting too long.

No wonder we are shocked when a wire story originating from a city in America informs that "a newborn girl who was wrapped in a paper bag and dumped in a garbage can is under close observation at a hospital. The child is doing well. 'She's a real beautiful, healthy baby,' a hospital spokesman said Wednesday. Police said the infant was discovered after trash men emptied the garbage can into the back end of their dump truck and saw something move in the debris. Authorities are looking for the mother."

It is our solemn duty, our precious privilege—even our sacred opportunity—to welcome to our homes and to our hearts the children who grace our lives.

Our children have three classrooms of learning which are quite distinct one from another. I speak of the classroom at school, the classroom in church, and the classroom called home.

The Church has always had a vital interest in public education and encourages its members to participate in parent-teacher activities and other events designed to improve the education of our youth.

There is no more important aspect of public education than the teacher who has the opportunity to love, to teach, and to inspire eager boys and girls and young men and young women. President David O. McKay said, "Teaching is the noblest profession in the world. Upon the proper education of youth depend the permanency and purity of home, the safety and perpetuity of the nation. The parent gives the child an opportunity to live; the teacher enables the child to live well." (*Gospel Ideals* [Salt Lake City: Improvement Era, 1953], p. 436.) I trust we shall recognize their importance and their vital mission by providing adequate facilities, the finest of books, and salaries which show our gratitude and our trust.

Each of us remembers with affection the teachers of our youth. I think it amusing that my elementary school music teacher was a Miss Sharp. She had the capacity to infuse within her pupils a love for music and taught us to identify musical instruments and their sounds. I well recall the influence of a Miss Ruth Crow who taught the subject of health. Though these were depression times, she ensured that each sixth-grade student had a dental health chart. She personally checked each pupil for dental health and made certain that through public or private resources, no child went without proper dental care. As Miss Burkhaus, who taught geography, rolled down the maps of the world and, with her pointer, marked the capital cities of nations and the distinctive features of each country, language, and culture, little did I anticipate or dream that one day I would visit those lands and peoples.

Oh, the importance in the lives of our children of teachers who lift their spirits, sharpen their intellects, and motivate their very lives!

The classroom at church adds a vital dimension to the education of every child and youth. In this setting each teacher can provide an upward reach to those who listen to the lessons and feel the influence of his or her testimony. In Primary, Sunday School, Young Women meetings and those of the Aaronic Priesthood, well-prepared teachers, called under the inspiration of the Lord, can touch each child, each youth, and prompt all to "seek . . . out of the best books words of wisdom; seek learning, even by study and also by faith." (D&C 88:118.) A word of encouragement here and a spiritual thought there can affect a precious life and leave an indelible imprint upon an immortal soul.

Many years ago, at a Church magazine awards banquet, we sat with President and Sister Harold B. Lee. President Lee said to our teenage daughter Ann, "The Lord has blessed you with a beautiful face and body. Keep the inside just as beautiful as the outside, and you will be blessed with true happiness." This master teacher left with Ann an inspired guide to the celestial kingdom of our Heavenly Father.

Humble and inspired teachers in the church classroom can instill in their pupils a love for the scriptures. Why, the teacher can bring the Apostles of old and the Savior of the world not only into the classroom but also into the hearts, the minds, the souls of our children.

Perhaps most significant of all classrooms is the classroom of the home. It is in the home that we form our attitudes, our deeply held beliefs. It is in the home that hope is fostered or destroyed. Our homes are the laboratories of our lives. What we do there determines the course of our lives when we leave home. Dr. Stuart E. Rosenberg wrote in his book *The Road to Confidence*, "Despite all new inventions and modern designs, fads and fetishes, no one has yet invented, or will ever invent, a satisfying substitute for one's own family."

A happy home is but an earlier heaven. President George Albert Smith asked, "Do we want our homes to be happy? If we do, let them be the abiding place of prayer, thanksgiving and gratitude." (In Conference Report, Apr. 1944, p. 32.)

There are those situations where children come to mortality with a physical or mental handicap. Try as we will, it is not possible to know why or how such events occur. I salute those parents who without complaint take such a child into their arms and into their lives and provide that added measure of sacrifice and love to one of Heavenly Father's children.

This past summer at Aspen Grove Family Camp, I observed a mother patiently feeding a teenage daughter injured at birth and totally dependent upon Mother. Mother administered each spoonful of food, each swallow of water, while holding steady the head and neck of her daughter. Silently I thought to myself, *For seventeen years, Mother has provided this service and all others to her daughter, never thinking of her own comfort, her own pleasure, her own food.* May God bless such mothers, such fathers, such children. And He will.

Parents everywhere realize that the most powerful combination of emotions in the world is not called out by any grand cosmic event, nor is it found in novels or history books, but merely by a parent gazing down upon a sleeping child.

When doing so, the truth of the words of Charles M. Dickenson come to mind:

> *They are idols of hearts and of households,*
> *They are angels of God in disguise;*
> *The sunlight still sleeps in their tresses,*
> *His glory still gleams in their eyes.*
> *These truants from home and from heaven,*
> *They have made me more manly and mild;*
> *And I know now how Jesus could liken*
> *The Kingdom of God to a child.*

In our daily experiences with children, we discover they are most perceptive and often utter profound truths. Charles Dickens, the author of the classic *A Christmas Carol*, illustrated this fact when he described the humble Bob Cratchit family assembling for a rather meager but long-anticipated Christmas dinner. Bob, the father, was returning home with his frail son Tiny Tim upon his shoulder. Tiny Tim "bore a little crutch, and had his limbs supported by an iron frame." Bob's wife asked of him, "And how did little Tim behave?"

"'As good as gold,' said Bob, 'and better. Somehow he gets thoughtful, sitting by himself so much, and thinks the strangest things you ever heard. He told me, coming home, that he hoped the people saw him in the church, because he was a cripple, and it might be pleasant to them to remember upon Christmas Day who made lame beggars walk, and blind men see.'" (*A Christmas Carol and Cricket on the Hearth* [New York: Grosset and Dunlop, n.d.], pp. 50–51.)

Charles Dickens himself said, "I love these little people, and it is not a slight thing when they who are so fresh from God love us."

Children express their love in original and innovative ways. On my birthday a few weeks ago, a precious little girl presented me with her handwritten birthday card and enclosed in the envelope a tiny toy padlock which she liked and thought I would enjoy receiving as a gift.

"Of all the dear sights in the world, nothing is so beautiful as a child when it is giving something. Any small thing it gives. A child gives the world to you. It opens the world to you as if it were a book you'd never been able to read. But when a gift must be found, it is always some absurd little thing, pasted on crooked, . . . an angel looking like a clown. A child has so little that it can give, because it never knows it has given you everything." (Margaret Lee Runbeck, *Bits & Pieces*, 20 Sept. 1990.)

Such was Jenny's gift to me.

Children seem to be endowed with abiding faith in their Heavenly Father and His capacity and desire to answer their sweet prayers. It has been my personal experience that when a child prays, God listens.

Let me share with you the experience of Barry Bonnell and Dale Murphy, well-known professional baseball players formerly with the Atlanta Braves baseball club. Each is a convert to the Church, Dale Murphy having been baptized by Barry Bonnell.

An experience occurred during the 1978 season that Barry described as "life changing." He was struggling terribly, batting about .200. Because of his poor performance, he was down on himself and felt miserable. He really didn't want to go when Dale Murphy asked him to "come along to the hospital," but he went anyway. There he met Ricky Little, a stalwart Atlanta Braves supporter, but a youngster afflicted with leukemia. It was readily apparent that Ricky was near death. Barry felt a deep desire to think of something comforting to say, but nothing seemed adequate. Finally, he asked if there were anything they could do. The youngster hesitated and then asked if they would each hit a home run for him during the next game. Barry said later, "That request wasn't such a hard thing for Dale, who in fact hit two homers that night, but I was struggling at the plate and hadn't hit a homer all year. Then I felt a warm feeling come over me, and I told Ricky to count on it." That night, Barry hit his only home run of the season. (Jim Ison, *Mormons in the Major Leagues.*) A child's prayer had been answered; a child's wish had been fulfilled.

If only all children had loving parents, safe homes, and caring friends, what a wonderful world would be theirs. Unfortunately, not all children are so bounteously blessed. Some children witness their fathers savagely beating their mothers, while others are on the receiving end of such abuse. What cowardice, what depravity, what shame!

Local hospitals everywhere receive these little ones, bruised and battered, accompanied by bald-faced lies that the child "ran into the door" or "fell down the stairs." Liars, bullies who abuse children, they will one day reap the whirlwind of their foul deeds. The quiet, the hurt, the offended child victim of abuse, and at times incest, must receive help.

A district judge, in a letter to me, declared, "Sexual abuse of children is one of the most depraved, destructive, and demoralizing crimes in civilized society. There is an alarming increase of reported physical, psychological, and sexual abuse of children. Our courts are becoming inundated with this repulsive behavior."

The Church does not condone such heinous and vile conduct. Rather, we condemn in the harshest of terms such treatment of God's precious children. Let the child be rescued, nurtured, loved, and healed. Let the offender be brought to justice, to accountability, for his actions and receive professional treatment to curtail such wicked and devilish conduct. When you and I know of such conduct and fail to take action to eradicate it, we become part of the problem. We share part of the guilt. We experience part of the punishment.

I trust I have not spoken too harshly, but I love these little ones and know that the Lord loves them, too. No more touching account of this love can be found than the experience of Jesus blessing the children as described in 3 Nephi. It tells of Jesus healing the sick, teaching the people, and praying to Heavenly Father for them. But then let me quote the precious words:

"[Jesus] took their little children, one by one, and blessed them, and prayed unto the Father for them.

"And when he had done this he wept again;

"And he spake unto the multitude, and said unto them: Behold your little ones.

"And as they looked to behold they cast their eyes towards heaven, and they saw the heavens open, and they saw angels descending out of heaven as it were in the midst of fire; . . . and the angels did minister unto them." (3 Nephi 17:21–24.)

You may ask: *Do such things occur even today?* Let me share with you the beautiful account of a grandmother and a grandfather now serving a mission and the manner in which their little grandson was blessed. The missionary grandfather wrote:

"My wife, Deanna, and I are now serving a mission in Jackson, Ohio. One of our big concerns as we accepted a mission call was our family. We would not be there when they had problems.

"Just before we went on our mission, our grandson, R.J., who was two and a half years old, had to have surgery to correct a crossed eye. His mother asked me to go with them because R.J. and I are real buddies. The operation went well, but R.J. did cry before and after the surgery because none of the family could go into the operating room, and he was afraid.

"About six months later, while we were still on our mission, R.J. needed the other eye corrected. His mother phoned and expressed her desire for me to be there to go with them for the second operation. Of course, distance and the mission prevented me from being with him. Deanna and I fasted and prayed for the Lord to comfort our grandson during his operation.

"We called shortly after the surgery was over and found that R.J. had remembered the previous experience and did not want to leave his parents. But as soon as he entered the operating room, he quieted down. He lay down on the operating table, took off his glasses for them, and went through the operation with a calm spirit. We were very thankful; our prayers had been answered.

"A couple of days later, we called our daughter and asked about R.J. He was doing fine, and she related this incident to us: In the afternoon after the operation, R.J. awakened and told his mother that Grandpa was there during the operation. He said, 'Grandpa was there and made it all right.' You see, the Lord made the anesthesiologist appear to that little boy as though he were his grandpa, but his grandpa and grandma were on a mission 1,800 miles away."

Grandpa may not have been by your bedside, R.J., but you were in his prayers and in his thoughts. You were cradled in the hand of the Lord and blessed by the Father of us all.

My dear brothers and sisters, may the laughter of children gladden our hearts. May the faith of children soothe our souls. May the love of children prompt our deeds. "Children are an heritage of the Lord." (Psalm 127:3.) May our Heavenly Father ever bless these sweet souls, these special friends of the Master, is my humble and earnest prayer.

From an address given at the October 1991 general conference while President Monson was serving as Second Counselor in the First Presidency. (See *Ensign*, Nov. 1991, pp. 67–70.)

Children at Peace

PRESIDENT MICHAELENE P. GRASSLI

Seven-year-old Jamie loved her mother dearly. The family had known for nearly a year that their wife and mother was dying of cancer. The father and seven children fasted and prayed; they pleaded with the Lord to heal her. Everything possible was done for their mother, yet at the end of three painfully difficult months, she passed from this life.

In the first hours following her death, the father brought the grieving family together. After prayer, the children went to their own rooms to prepare for bed. Jamie, who had spent many hours with her mother and was devoted to her, knelt at her own bedside. "Heavenly Father," she prayed through her tears, "we thank thee for the great mom you gave us. We thank thee for helping us try to make her well. Help us to be good so we can live with her again." Without a hint of bitterness, this little seven-year-old girl continued for several minutes in a sweet attitude of peaceful prayer, reflecting her understanding and acceptance of her mother's death.

Jamie was a child at peace. How did she come to that peace? She had been prepared by parents with spiritual understanding. Such preparation brings peace.

I have chosen to speak about our children—precious children of our Heavenly Father throughout the earth. I pray that my message will be received and understood, for these are among the most valiant spirits to come into the world. We can do no less than to bestow on them a legacy of peace.

Our Heavenly Father has promised peace to His children. "All thy children shall be taught of the Lord; and great shall be the peace of thy children." (3 Nephi 22:13.) Peace in the Lord can give them freedom from self-doubt, freedom from fear, freedom from the confinement of their environment, freedom from enslaving habits. His peace can free them to unfold from the tender buds they are to the mature and fruitful adults they can be.

Just as the fragile bud contains all of the essential elements to develop into a lovely plant or flower, so does each child come to us with the potential for individual self-fulfillment of his eternal destiny. In both instances, in order for what is inside to be fully developed, it must be nurtured from the outside. In nature, plants require light, water, air, and nutrients to thrive. The human spirit thrives on love, knowledge of its origin, and teachings of a spiritual nature. It is important that we provide a favorable environment for spiritual growth and the peace that will accompany it. This peace I speak of will result in quiet assurances even in the midst of worldly pressures and turmoil.

Brothers and sisters, the children need our help. They need us to prepare them. They need us to help them obtain the peace of the Lord. Today is neither too early nor too late to prepare the children, and anyone can do it. A young, new family just beginning; an established family with children of several ages; a family with one parent; grandparents, aunts, uncles, neighbors; and kind, understanding Church leaders and teachers—all of us can teach children of the Lord.

We begin by teaching what we are. The children need us; they need to see in us what they can become. They need to see us keeping the commandments. *We* must come unto the Lord and seek for the peace of the gospel in *our own* lives. "Learn of me," the Lord said, "and listen to my words; walk in the meekness of my Spirit, and you shall have peace in me." (D&C 19:23.) When we are at peace, then our children can be at peace.

A wise bishop made this observation: "I have seen families where parents are at home with the gospel, where gospel principles are a matter-of-fact, everyday way of life, where parents treat their children with courtesy and respect with the full understanding that they are children of God. In these homes, the children seem to be at peace because their parents have given them a clear message. They know they are children of God. They feel their worth and have focus to their lives, knowing that eternity is their goal."

To some, a family like the ones described by that bishop may seem impossible to attain. No family is perfect—all families are made up of human beings with mortal weaknesses, who sometimes go astray. But family members, including parents, can begin where they are and learn and grow together.

Now, we have been promised that family home evening, family prayer, and reading the scriptures together can strengthen and give direction to each member of a family and can knit the family together. If you haven't been having family home evening or family prayer, you may feel awkward about beginning. That's all right. Do it anyway. Gather the family together; tell them that although you haven't been doing so, you want to begin.

Now, I must warn you that Satan will attempt to thwart your efforts because family strength is a threat to his work. So persevere, even though it takes some effort and planning to overcome attitudes and obstacles.

When the family gathers for evening prayer, it is a good time for sharing the day's experiences, reading the scriptures, and sharing testimonies. Children especially need to hear the testimonies of their parents. One family repeats one article of faith every evening for a week, or memorizes a scripture, or recites the names of the books in the Book of

Mormon. Another family focuses on one child or a parent each day with each member telling something good about that person. It takes just a few minutes. Children of all ages need to hear positive observations about themselves—especially from their parents.

Immerse the children in the stories of Jesus so that they can know Him and can imagine what it might have been like to have lived when He was on the earth. Tell them how He took the children on His knee and blessed them and prayed for them. Tell them how the people knew He was the Son of God.

When I was a child I loved to hear about the Savior's triumphal entry into Jerusalem. Many people heard Jesus was coming to Jerusalem for the Feast of the Passover. They knew He was the Son of God. They went out to meet Him. Imagine what it must have been like to be a child in that happy crowd. The scripture says it was "a very great multitude." (Matthew 21:8.) They were probably waiting along the narrow streets of Jerusalem becoming more and more excited as they strained to see if He was coming yet. Then as He came into view, riding on a donkey, can't you just hear a great cheer going up? They spread their clothes and tree branches on the ground for the donkey to walk on, as they did for kings, and they waved palm leaves in the air. They cried, "Hosanna to the Son of David . . . Hosanna in the highest." (Matthew 21:9.) Oh, wouldn't you love to have been there?

Yes, tell them about the Savior so they'll trust Him, so they'll develop a desire to be like Him and want to be with Him again. Yes, our homes can provide peace for the children. Blessings be on you parents.

And blessings be on you devoted Church leaders who hold the welfare and spiritual growth of children in high priority—priesthood and Primary leaders who minister to the children. At Primary, children are taught of the Lord. A wise stake Primary president in Australia has as her goal that when the children come to Primary, they will feel the Spirit of the Lord. Those will be children at peace.

President Benson, I'm proud to say that Primary children have this year read and discussed the Book of Mormon. Nine-year-old Matt in Wisconsin spoke in the Children's Sacrament Meeting Presentation in his ward recently about something he had learned that brought him peace. He said:

"When my father told our family that we would be moving from Denver to Wisconsin, my mother reminded us of Lehi's family. Like them, I was leaving the only home I had known, all my friends, my school, and my ward. Luckily *we* got to bring all our possessions with us, though they were in storage for three months, and we missed having a house and our 'precious things.'

"My mother reminded us of how Nephi accepted this challenge—willingly—knowing that the Lord would 'prepare a way for them that they may accomplish the thing which he commandeth them.' (See 1 Nephi 3:7.)

"I have learned that I can do without things, but not without my family. My brothers and sisters and I have tried to be more like Nephi than his complaining brothers. I am grateful for the things that the Book of Mormon teaches us."

Yes, when children are taught of the Lord, we bestow on them a gift, a legacy of peace, that can lead them to eternal life. We must not fail them. May all our children have the blessing to be taught of the Lord that they might be, indeed, children at peace.

From an address given at the October 1988 general conference while President Grassli was serving as Primary General President. (See *Ensign*, Nov. 1988, pp. 78–79.)

The Power of Family Prayer

ELDER JOHN H. GROBERG

Our Father in Heaven wants us to have strong, loving families. One of the great helps He has given us to achieve this is family prayer. It is a vitally important key to our happiness and success in life.

All of us, single or married, are eternally part of some family—someway, somewhere, somehow—and much of our joy in life comes as we correctly recognize and properly develop those family relationships. We come to this earth charged with a mission: to learn to love and serve one another. To best help us accomplish this, God has placed us in families, for He knows that is where we can best learn to overcome selfishness and pride and to sacrifice for others and to make happiness and helpfulness and humility and love the very essence of our character.

We learn that friends and neighbors come and go but family is forever, and as we learn this, we find that we are eternally our brother's keeper and we begin to realize how much help we need. How we should thank God for the opportunity of family prayer!

Listen to the admonition of the Savior in Third Nephi: "Pray in your families unto the Father, always in my name, that your wives and your children may be blessed." (3 Nephi 18:21.)

Can you detect that if we do not pray in our families always they may not be blessed—or at least not so fully? If we truly love our families, we will constantly pray for them and with them. I know of no single activity that has more potential for unifying our families and bringing more love and divine direction into our homes than consistent, fervent family prayer.

Think of the power for good as you gather your family together and thank God for all of His blessings. Think of the eternal significance of daily thanking Him for each member of your family and asking Him to guide and bless and protect each one. Think of the strength that will come to your family as, daily, one member or another pours out his or her soul in love to God for other family members.

Of course, our prayers must be more than words, for as President Marion G. Romney has so clearly stated, "The efficacy of our prayers depends on how we care for one another." (*Ensign*, Nov. 1980, p. 93.) Family prayer is fully effective, then, only as we rise from our knees and, with increased love and understanding, take better care of each other.

We all want more love and unity in our families. We all need more help with some who may be wayward or in special need. We all desire more assurance of divine guidance and direction.

I promise you that as you consistently and fervently pray as a family, and as each member takes his or her turn and sincerely prays for others, impressions will come as to what you individually should do to help others. Thus, you can, in family prayer, receive personal and family revelation as to how to love and serve one another.

Now, Satan will do everything he can to keep us from family prayer, or at least to see that our prayers are only intermittent and mechanical and without sincerity. In Daniel's day, Satan influenced evil men to pass laws against praying. In our day, Satan's efforts seem a little more subtle (although he is trying a little of that law business, too).

But remember, the greatest schools on earth are individual homes. Yet how many homes voluntarily give up family prayer by allowing other, less-important things to take priority.

If Satan can get us thinking that our children are too young or too old, or if he can get us angry with one another or preoccupied with TV programs or overcrowded schedules or caught up in some other aspect of the press of modern life so that we do not have family prayer, he has effectively won on that point—even though many of the other things we do may be good in and of themselves.

Satan doesn't care how he stops us—just so he stops us. Ask yourself: How many times did you have family prayer this last week? Who is winning in your home? What's the score? Don't let the evil one win. You can overcome him with God's help.

I appeal with all the fervor of my soul to every family in the Church, every family in the nation, every family in the world, to organize your priorities so that God is first in your lives and to show this by having regular family prayer. There may be extenuating circumstances occasionally; but as a rule, we should have family prayer every morning and every evening.

Oh, if we would do this, if we would show our families and our God on a regular basis how much we love them, how much we appreciate them, how much we need their help, and how much we rely on His protection, one of the greatest changes for good to ever take place in the Church, in the nation, and in the world would occur. Don't let anything stand in the way of consistent, fervent family prayer! Think of what you teach by having family prayer. Then think of what you teach by not having family prayer.

I testify to you that there is real power in family prayer. I testify that families can be brought together and can help and strengthen one another through family prayer.

Let me illustrate this with an incident that happened some years ago. As a young man I was called on a mission to Tonga. Through a series of unusual circumstances, such as ship strikes, and so forth, it took three months to get to Tonga from Salt Lake. As I was the only one assigned to Tonga at that time, much of the journey was made alone.

In Samoa, the mission president put me on a boat to Fiji and assured me that he would telegraph ahead, and when I arrived in Suva two elders would meet me and put me on a boat to Tonga.

Even though I had been in transit for two and a half months at that time, that several-day voyage to Suva seemed extra-filled with trepidation. How I looked forward to seeing those two missionaries!

The boat arrived in Suva early in the morning. I looked and looked but could see no elders. An hour went by, then two, then three—still no elders. The captain kept telling me to get off the boat as they were leaving soon. I kept telling him that I would be met soon by two young men, but they didn't come.

Finally, noon arrived and the captain was ready to leave. "Get off," he said. "You only have a ticket to Suva. I'm leaving, and you're staying here."

With great fear I started down the gangplank only to be met by the immigration officials. "Let us see your visa, your onward ticket, and the money to keep you while here," they demanded.

I had no visa. I had no onward ticket. I had not sufficient money. But I assured them that two young men would be there right away with whatever was needed. How I prayed! But they didn't come.

"Back on the ship then," they insisted.

"Not on my ship," bellowed the captain.

I can remember standing in the middle of the gangplank, looking up at the folded arms and glaring eyes of the stern captain and then looking down at the equally determined faces and set jaws of the immigration men.

I looked at the ocean under the gangplank. I should

have wondered how long I could tread water, but I was too scared to think of anything right then.

In the end, the captain proved to be the toughest; and amidst cursing and yelling and banging of bags, the gangplank went up, the ship departed, and I found myself in the not-too-friendly hands of the immigration officials.

There was a long discussion among them, most of it in a foreign tongue. Finally, one of the younger men, who seemed more friendly, came over and explained that for now I should move with my things into the "customs shed." That's where things go that aren't really allowed into the country until duty or tax is paid on them. He assured me that he, too, felt that the two young men I referred to would soon be along and everything would be fine.

The afternoon wore on. I tried several times to contact the missionaries every way I knew how but to no avail. I know missionaries are supposed to be brave, but right then I was scared and tired and hungry.

The sun was getting low, and it seemed the lower it got in the sky the lower my spirits became. I knew I wasn't really in danger or in prison, but to one used to lots of freedom it seemed like it.

The pungent odor of curry and copra and drying fish and the myriad other sights and sounds and smells of an oily tropical wharf seemed so foreign to the cool, fresh smells of my Idaho home. I knew I was homesick. I wanted to cry, but I knew that wouldn't do any good.

Finally, the whirring of winches, the groaning of blocks and cables, the banging of cargo, and the sputtering of machines ceased. The dock workers began to leave, and then the immigration people, until just a few watchmen and supervisors were left. It was silent now. I don't know when I have felt more alone.

I tried to lie down on the dirty, uneven cement floor. I prayed to know what to do. There seemed to be no answer. I watched the last rays of sunlight as they broke through the clouds and blazed across the ocean and through the holes of the metal customs shed.

"How long will the light last?" I thought. Then I wondered, "What will happen when those last rays disappear and fold into the night?" (Have you ever wanted to just sort of close your eyes and disappear—or have things around you change?) "But, no, I must have hope. Things *must* turn out all right."

Once more, I closed my eyes in prayer, when suddenly I felt almost transported. I didn't see anything or hear anything, in a physical sense; but, in a more real way, I saw a family in far-off Idaho kneeling together in prayer; and I heard my mother, acting as mouth, say as clearly as anything can be heard, "And bless John on his mission."

As that faithful family called down the powers of heaven to bless their missionary son in a way they could not physically do, I testify that the powers of heaven did come down, and they lifted me up and, in a spiritual way, allowed me, for a brief moment, to once again join that family circle in prayer. I was one with them. I was literally swallowed up in the love and concern of a faithful family and sensed for a moment what being taken into Abraham's bosom may be like. (See Luke 16:22.) I was given to understand also that there are other circles of love and concern unbounded by time or space to which we all belong and from which we can draw strength. God does not leave us entirely alone—ever!

Tears of joy flowed freely as I had restored to me the warmth of security, the light of love, and the strength of hope. And when I again felt the hard, uneven cement beneath me, there was no fear, no sorrow, no trepidation, only deep gratitude and certain assurance.

To conclude the incident, within a half hour I saw the young immigration man who had befriended me coming towards the shed with two young elders behind him. It seemed that on his way home he just happened to run into two young Americans with white shirts and ties and told them about one just like them down at the wharf. Apparently the telegram never arrived, but they followed him down to the shed, and soon all was straightened out, and within a few weeks I landed in Tonga and was ready to begin my mission.

Brothers and sisters, I testify that there is great power in loving, consistent, fervent family prayer. Don't deny your family this blessing. Don't allow the strength that comes from family prayer to slip away from you and your loved ones through neglect.

No matter what other inheritance you leave your family, give them the inheritance of knowing through experience that, forever, you will be praying for them and they for you.

Call your family together. Make your family prayers a top priority item. It may be awkward at first, if you aren't doing it now; and since Satan doesn't want you to do it at all, he will throw all sorts of excuses and roadblocks at you; but just proceed and be persistent, and I promise you great blessings.

Remember, all that we are commanded to do in this life is patterned after that of a better life. Do you think it a strange thought that maybe part of the power of family prayer is in the fact that we are part of a heavenly family, that they are interested in us, and that by tying in with them some way we get hold of something much bigger than ourselves?

Think of the power of the thousands of prayers of parents and grandparents and back and back even to Jacob and Isaac and Abraham and beyond, all requesting essentially the same thing: "Bless my children. Bless my children. Bless my children." Can you hear it as it rolls and echoes throughout all eternity?

Let us all be part of that great power for good.

I testify that time and space are no barriers to these righteous influences, and no matter where we are or what our situation is—even in the depths of discouragement, far from our loved ones—we too can feel and be strengthened by those soul-stirring words, "and bless John or Jane or whomever on his or her mission," for indeed life is a mission. We are all here on assignment to learn to love and serve one another; and we can't do this as well as we should unless we have consistent, fervent family prayer.

I testify that God is our Father, that He lives and loves us, that He is the Giver of all good things. I testify that Jesus lives and loves us, that He is the Son of God, the Christ, the Savior of the world, the head of this, His church. I testify that as we pray to the Father, in His name, all things are possible.

May we all gather our families around us and consistently and fervently pray for one another and thus, in righteousness, feel the needs of others and then fill the needs of others, thereby fulfilling much of our mission in life.

From an address given at the April 1982 general conference while Elder Groberg was serving as a member of the Seventy. (See *Ensign*, May 1982, pp. 50–52.)

Teaching Children
the Joy of Honest Labor

ELDER L. TOM PERRY

In Proverbs we read, "Train up a child in the way he should go: and when he is old, he will not depart from it." (Proverbs 22:6.)

One of the great challenges of life for parents from the very beginning has been succeeding in the very important task of rearing children. This great responsibility seems destined to bring the greatest joys and some of the greatest sorrows life has in store for us here in mortality.

Every child, of course, is different, and what works for one may not elicit the correct response from another. However, I believe that second only to ensuring that every child receives an understanding of the gospel of our Lord and Savior is teaching each one the joy of honest labor.

I was taught this by goodly parents. How grateful I am for a father who had the patience to teach me how to work. I remember that as a lad, when I was only seven years old, we were remodeling our house and tearing out some of the walls. In those days two-by-sixes were used as studding. To the studs was nailed the lath, and over the lath came the plaster. When one was tearing out walls, the slats and the plaster were easy to knock off, but, of course, that left the nails in the two-by-sixes.

Each night after the workers had finished, I had the responsibility of gathering up the two-by-sixes and taking them out to the back lawn, where there stood two sawhorses.

81

There I was to make a pile of the two-by-sixes and then, one at a time, put them on the sawhorses and with a crowbar remove the nails. After the nails had been pulled out of the studs, I was told to straighten them. Finally, I threw the straightened nails into a large green bucket and stacked the two-by-sixes in a neat pile.

There was so much in this project that was of value to me in my young life. First, I was taught to be productive, to work, to be busily engaged, and not to waste my time in idleness.

From the very beginning, the Lord commanded Adam to till the earth and have dominion over the beasts of the field, to eat his bread by the sweat of his brow. I have always been interested in how often the scriptures have admonished us to cease to be idle and to be productive in all of our labors. King Benjamin in his final address noted his example before the people by saying:

"I say unto you that as I have been suffered to spend my days in your service, even up to this time, and have not sought gold nor silver nor any manner of riches of you. . . .

"And even I, myself, have labored with mine own hands that I might serve you, and that ye should not be laden with taxes, and that there should nothing come upon you which was grievous to be borne—and of all these things which I have spoken, ye yourselves are witnesses this day." (Mosiah 2:12, 14.)

Teaching children the joy of honest labor is one of the greatest of all gifts you can bestow upon them. I am convinced that one of the reasons for the breakup of so many couples today is the failure of parents to teach and train sons in their responsibility to provide and care for their families and to enjoy the challenge this responsibility brings. Many of us also have fallen short in instilling within our daughters the desire of bringing beauty and order into their homes through homemaking.

Oh, how essential it is that children be taught early in

life the joy that comes from starting and fashioning a job that is the workmanship of their own hands. Teach children the joy of honest labor. Provide a foundation for life that builds confidence and fulfillment in each life. "Happy is the man who has work he loves to do. . . . Happy is the man who loves the work he has to do." (Anonymous.)

Second, as a lad doing the job my father had assigned to me, I was taught not to waste, to conserve resources where possible. When the nails were pulled from them, the two-by-sixes could be used again—and we did use them.

I have always enjoyed reading some of the counsel Brigham Young used to give to the Saints. His counsel was so practical. Listen to what he said about waste:

"Pick up everything. . . .

"Never consider that you have bread enough around you to suffer your children to waste a crust or a crumb of it. . . . Remember it, do not waste anything, but take care of everything.

"If you wish to get rich, save what you get. A fool can earn money: but it takes a wise man to save and dispose of it to his own advantage." (*Discourses of Brigham Young,* sel. John A. Widtsoe [Salt Lake City: Deseret Book Co., 1944], p. 292.)

I wonder what kind of signals we are sending to our children when we purchase homes that are status symbols. We waste space and resources when we buy a larger home than is needed, a larger home than is practical for us to afford. We encumber ourselves with mortgages so large that they require the income of both husband and wife to make payments. Then we build consumer debt to the point of absorbing completely all of our disposable income, leaving no margin of safety for the rainy days that come into every-one's life. Do not such signals from heads of households only feed the philosophy of "I want it now" in the lives of our children?

Some even have the mistaken belief that after turning

their ears away from the counsel of the prophets to avoid unnecessary debt, they can then turn to their bishops to bail them out of their foolishness. About all the poor bishops can do is weep with them and help them move to more affordable housing and then counsel them on how they can cut their losses.

As I remember events in my life, I do not believe there was any degree of difference in the happiness that I enjoyed when my two brothers and I shared a single bedroom than when we had a home large enough that each of us enjoyed a bedroom. Let us teach our children the art of conservation and the elimination of wastefulness.

Third, I will never forget my consternation as I watched the workmen using new nails as they built the walls back up and completed remodeling our home. The pile of nails that I had straightened and put in the green bucket grew and grew and was never used. I went to my father and said, "Wouldn't it be better to save the new nails and use the ones I have straightened?" I was proud of the work I had accomplished.

My father showed me something very important. He took a new nail and using an odd angle, drove it into a board. He was able to drive it straight and true. Then he took one of the nails I had straightened so carefully and, using the same odd angle, hit it again and again. It soon bent and was impossible to drive into the board. So I learned that a used, or bent, nail, is never as strong as a new one. But then why had my father asked me to straighten those nails?

As a boy, I never remember receiving a satisfactory answer. It was not until I had a son of my own that I started to understand. When my son was about three years old, I took him out to the garden to help me weed. I assumed that he, being low to the ground at the time, would have a real advantage at weeding. Unfortunately for my garden, he had a difficult time distinguishing between the weeds and the young plants.

I then tried Lee at milking a cow we owned together with a neighbor. He quickly developed the hand action of a fine milker, but, sadly, his aim was not very good. Whenever I checked on him, he was always surrounded by a white puddle, and the milk bucket was nearly empty. He would look up at me and smile proudly, and my initial inclination to be angry would quickly dissipate—but I was frustrated. I expected him to help me, but he only seemed to create more work.

It was in such moments of frustration that I remembered straightening the nails for my father, and I began to understand. Work is something more than the final end result. It is a *discipline*. We must learn to do, and do well, before we can expect to receive tangible rewards for our labors. My father must have known that if he focused on the outcome of my labors, he would only become frustrated with how inadequately I did things then. So he found tasks that were difficult and would challenge me, to teach me the discipline of hard work. He was using the straightened nails not to rebuild our home but to build my character.

Finally, I was instructed to stack the used two-by-sixes in a neat pile so the workmen could use them the next day. My work was never finished until this was done and the tools were put away.

Let us also teach our children to see that the work assigned is carried to its completion, to take pride in what they accomplish. There is a real satisfaction that comes from finishing a task, especially when it is the best work we know how to do.

These lessons instilled in me a joy and appreciation for honest labor and prepared me for that time in my life when I would have the responsibility of providing for a family. The principles I was taught by my wise father of honest labor, of not wasting, of discipline, and of seeing a task to its completion were basic to my success in any profession I might choose to follow. These lessons placed me in a position to face with confidence the challenges of an ever-changing world.

Is this not the same lesson that Paul was preaching when he declared:

"Neither did we eat any man's bread for nought; but wrought with labour and travail night and day, that we might not be chargeable to any of you:

"Not because we have not power, but to make ourselves an ensample unto you to follow us." (2 Thessalonians 3:8–9.)

An event occurred in my life about a month ago which impressed upon me the blessings that accrue to one over the years from good, early childhood training. I was delivered a note as I arrived at the airport that one of my very best friends had passed away and her funeral was in just an hour and a half in a community fifty miles from the airport. I made a quick change from air to surface transportation and started the drive to the funeral.

This great soul who had just passed away had been my Primary teacher for three years during my days as a Trail Builder when I was eight, nine, and ten years old. As I drove to Sister Call's funeral that morning, my mind was flooded with pleasant memories of my early childhood.

I especially remembered the powerful example of early childhood training—goodly parents who were always there to teach, inspire, love, and give strong encouragement to help me chart the right course in my life. I remembered a kind aunt who lived next door, who fortified and provided a second witness to the teachings of my parents.

Then I remembered dear Sister Call, a Primary teacher who extended herself much beyond her classroom call. Her lessons included many field trips to teach us of life, labor, and the joy of association. Her special way of weaving her lessons into our lives gave us an understanding of our personal worth.

As I drove along the highway, my heart was filled with overwhelming gratitude for parents, extended family, and Church leaders who had the patience, love, and concern to build a foundation in the life of a child during those very critical years.

Should not *all* children receive such a blessing early in their lives? This is the Lord's work in which we are engaged. He has charted the course and revealed the fundamental principles that will lead us back to His presence. May we have the strength and the courage to follow Him.

_____

From an address given at the October 1986 general conference while Elder Perry was serving as a member of the Quorum of the Twelve Apostles. (See *Ensign*, Nov. 1986, pp. 62–64.)

Rearing Children in a Polluted Environment

ELDER JOE J. CHRISTENSEN

Not long ago, I had an impromptu conversation with a group of young parents who exhibited a great deal of anxiety about rearing their children in our morally polluted environment. They asked for assistance in helping their children find their way in a world that seems to be unraveling.

We all hear and read a great deal these days about our polluted physical environment—acid rain, smog, toxic wastes. But these parents recognize that there is another kind of pollution that is much more dangerous—the moral and spiritual.

In a recent conference, Elder Boyd K. Packer said, "As we test the *moral* environment, we find the *pollution* index is spiraling upward." (*Ensign,* May 1992, p. 66.) The Apostle Paul foresaw "that in the last days perilous times shall come." (2 Timothy 3:1.) And speaking of the last days, the prophet Moroni declared, "Yea, it shall come in a day when there shall be great pollutions upon the face of the earth." (Mormon 8:31.)

Sadly, the effects of this great pollution are perhaps most evident in the mass media, films, television, and popular music. Of this, Senator Robert D. Byrd said: "If we in this nation continue to sow the images of murder, violence, drug abuse, . . . perversion, [and] pornography . . . before the eyes of millions of children, year after year and day after day, we should not be surprised if the foundations of our society rot away as if from leprosy." (Michael Medved, *Hollywood vs. America* [New York: Harper Perennial, 1992], p. 194.)

Although there are some uplifting exceptions, in most areas of the mass media there seems to be a declaration of war against almost everything the majority treasures most: the family, religion, and patriotism. Marriage is degraded, while premarital and extramarital relations are encouraged and glamorized. Profanity and the foulest of vulgar gutter language bombard the ears of all who listen. Reportedly, in one R-rated movie, the most common, vulgar, four-letter word was spoken 256 times! Human life itself is trivialized by the constant barrage of violence and killings. Remember that anything that is not good for children is rarely good for adults.

In an unsuccessful effort to ward off teen pregnancy and social disease, birth control devices are freely distributed. I am convinced that this practice strongly communicates the basic message to many youth that "anything goes; just protect yourself in the process."

It is no wonder that young parents become very anxious as they attempt to fulfill their sacred trust in the face of such an onslaught of despicable influences. Unfortunately, these challenges confront members of the Church as well as non-members.

Parents who really want to receive assistance must return to the basics—the fundamentals of the gospel. Among all that could be said, here are four specific suggestions that, if applied, can make a positive difference:

First, *do not be afraid to set clear moral standards and guidelines.* Be sure to say no when it is needed. As Dr. John Rosemond counseled:

"[Give] your children regular, daily doses of Vitamin N. This vital nutrient consists simply of the most character-building two-letter word in the English language [*No*]. . . .

Unfortunately, many, if not most, of today's children suffer from Vitamin N deficiency. They've been overindulged by well-meaning parents who've given them far too much of what they want and far too little of what they truly need." (*John Rosemond's Six-Point Plan for Raising Happy, Healthy Children* [Kansas City, Mo.: Andrews & McMeel, 1989], p. 114.)

Even though your children say, "Well, everyone else is going to stay out until one or two in the morning, and their parents don't care. Why can't I? Don't you trust me?" let them know that there are some things that members of your family simply do not do. Some parents seem to be almost pathologically concerned about their children's popularity and social acceptance and go along with many things that are really against their better judgment, such as expensive fads, immodest clothes, late hours, dating before age sixteen, R-rated movies, and so on. For children and parents, standing up for what is right may be lonely at times. There may be evenings alone, parties missed, and movies which go unseen. It may not always be fun. But parenting is not a popularity contest.

You may need to get together with the parents of your children's friends and mutually agree on more acceptable, high standards of entertainment, hours, and activities. Your children may be frustrated at first, but in the end they will grow to appreciate you even more because you cared enough about them to set some wholesome guidelines and standards.

Second, *teach your children to work and to take responsibility.* Especially in urban settings, too many children are growing up in an environment where they do not have enough to do. They are like the young thirteen-year-old boy who was asked what he did all day in the summer.

He said, "Well, I get up in the morning about ten or eleven. Then my mom gets me something to eat. Then maybe, I'll go with some of the guys and play a little basketball, maybe watch TV, and then go down to the mall and 'hang out' for a while—sorta watch the girls and stuff."

When asked what time he got to bed, he said, "Oh, usually about one or two o'clock. I go over to a friend's house and watch some videos. It's really neat, because my friend's mom told the guy at the video shop that it was all right for her son to check out any video he wanted—including R-rated."

I feel great concern for the future of that young Latter-day Saint boy as well as for that of his friends.

I like what President Spencer W. Kimball has said on this topic:

"The idle generation! Hours each day and nothing to do. . . .

"We want you parents to create work for your children. . . .

" 'What can we do?' they ask.

"Do the shopping, work in the hospital, help the neighbors and the church custodian, wash dishes, vacuum the floors, make the beds, get the meals, learn to sew.

"Read good books, . . . clean the house, press your clothes, rake the leaves, shovel the snow, peddle papers."

Then he concludes:

"Lawmakers in their overeagerness to protect the child have legislated until the pendulum has swung to the other extreme. But no law prohibits most work [here] suggested . . . , and parents can make work." (*The Teachings of Spencer W. Kimball,* ed. Edward L. Kimball [Salt Lake City: Bookcraft, 1982], pp. 360–61.)

In addition, help your children learn self-discipline by such activities as learning to play a musical instrument or other demanding skill. I am reminded of the story of the salesman who came to a house one hot summer day. Through the screen door, he could see a young boy practicing his scales on the piano. His baseball glove and hat were by the side of the piano bench. He said, "Say, boy, is your mother home?" To which the boy replied, "What do you think?" Thank heavens for conscientious parents!

Every child should be helped to develop some skill or talent by which he or she can experience success and thus build self-esteem.

Missionaries who have learned to work hard and have developed self-discipline are much more successful.

Third, *create an environment in your family in which spiritual experiences can occur.* For example:

Hold family home evenings *every week* without fail. This is a wonderful time to share your testimony with your children. Give them an opportunity to share their feelings about the gospel. Help them learn to recognize when they feel the presence of the Spirit. Family home evenings will help create an island of refuge and security within your own home.

Read the scriptures together daily as a family. There is real power in the scriptures.

President Benson has said, "May I admonish you to participate in a program of daily reading and pondering of the scriptures. . . . The Book of Mormon will change your life. It will fortify you against the evils of our day. It will bring a spirituality into your life that no other book will." (*Ensign,* May 1986, p. 43.)

Is the Book of Mormon a significant part of your reading? Count the number of rich promises President Marion G. Romney made to parents when he said:

"I feel certain that if, in our homes, parents will read from the Book of Mormon prayerfully and regularly, both by themselves and with their children, the spirit of that great book will come to permeate our homes. . . . The spirit of reverence will increase; mutual respect and consideration for each other will grow. The spirit of contention will depart. Parents will counsel their children in greater love and wisdom. Children will be more responsive and submissive to the counsel of their parents. Righteousness will increase. . . . The pure love of Christ . . . will abound in our homes and lives, bringing in their wake peace, joy, and happiness." (*Ensign,* May 1980, p. 67.)

We should not take these ten promises lightly.

Fourth, *follow the counsel of the prophets.* Listen to their messages at this conference and reread their counsel to us from prior occasions. If your personal and family practices do not conform to the counsel received, then, for your own family's sake, make some changes.

President Harold B. Lee said: "We must learn to give heed to the words and commandments that the Lord shall give through his prophet . . . [and quoting from the Doctrine and Covenants] 'as if from mine own mouth, in all patience and faith' (D&C 21:4–5)." He continued: "There will be some things that take patience and faith. You may not like what comes from the authority of the Church. It may contradict your political views. It may contradict your social views. It may interfere with some of your social life. . . . Your safety and ours depends upon whether or not we follow the ones whom the Lord has placed to preside over his church." (In Conference Report, Oct. 1970, pp. 152–53.)

From a personal standpoint, of what value is it to have living prophets if we do not heed their counsel?

Fathers and mothers, it is not too late to change. There is still hope. You can begin today to apply these suggestions and others you may add. We can help our children and grandchildren to survive spiritually and morally in a world where the pollution index continues to spiral upward. The intent is not to take our children out of the world but, as the Lord prayed, to keep them from evil. (See John 17:15.)

From an address given at the October 1993 general conference while Elder Christensen was serving as a member of the Presidency of the Seventy. (See *Ensign,* Nov. 1993, pp. 11–13.)

Ward and Branch Families: Part of Heavenly Father's Plan for Us

SISTER VIRGINIA H. PEARCE

I believe that Heavenly Father recognized that even though our relationship with Him and our accountability to Him are intensely personal, we gather strength when we meet in groups. We need to be reminded often that we are a part of something big and grand as we continue to do our own part. Each Sunday in gatherings around the world, young women stand and say aloud together: not "*I*" but "*We* are daughters of *our* Heavenly Father who loves *us*, and *we* love him. *We* will 'stand as witnesses' . . . " and so on. (Young Women Theme; emphasis added.)

Learning in groups is so important that Heavenly Father planned for us to be born into a group—the most basic, most hallowed, and most powerful group on earth: the family. We have heard good counsel about the family. I would like to build on that by talking about the *ward* or *branch* family—the basic ecclesiastical unit to which we all belong as members of the Church of Jesus Christ. For simplicity, I will use the word *ward* to include both wards and branches, since they both serve the same purposes. Wards are designed not to replace the family unit but to support the family and its righteous teachings. A ward is another place where there is enough commitment and energy to form a sort of "safety net" family for each of us when our families cannot or do not provide all of the teaching and growing experiences we need to return to Heavenly Father.

It is my desire and prayer that we will expand our appreciation of the power of the ward family and renew our commitment to participate positively in that community of Saints.

First, ward families provide a sense of belonging. Robert Frost said in his narrative poem "The Death of the Hired Man" (lines 118–20):

> *Home is the place where, when you have to go there,*
> *They have to take you in.*
> *I should have called it*
> *Something you somehow haven't to deserve.*

A ward is "something you somehow haven't to deserve." Membership in the Church of Jesus Christ gives us that home. In a ward, as in a family, every person is different and valuable. Paul said:

"For by one Spirit are we all baptized into one body, whether we be Jews or Gentiles, whether we be bond or free; . . .

"For the body is not one member, but many." (1 Corinthians 12:13–14.) The Savior instructed that we should meet together often and forbid no one. (See 3 Nephi 18:22.)

Several months ago while visiting our children in another state, I walked with our two-and-a-half-year-old grandson from the chapel to the nursery. As he moved rather energetically down the hall, at least five people called him by name—teenagers, children, adults. "Hi, Benjamin," "Hey, Benjamin," "Morning, Benjamin." My heart overflowed with gratitude that Benjamin is learning that he, as an individual, belongs to a ward family. Over a lifetime, ward families will do for him what his family alone cannot do.

In the April 1992 general conference, Young Women General President Janette C. Hales asked adult members to "learn the names of the young people in [their] ward or branch and call them by name." (*Ensign*, May 1992, p. 80.)

Now, I would enlarge her invitation, inviting you young men and young women to learn the names of the adults and the children. Overcome your natural timidity and greet as many people as you can by name each week. Our wards will be better places if, like Benjamin, everyone hears his own name four or five times between the chapel and the classroom. We can each help that to happen.

Next, ward families provide the reassurance of listening ears. Someone has said that people would rather be understood than be loved. In truth, the surest way to increase our love for someone is to listen with patience and respect. I believe that our baptismal covenant demands this. How can we "mourn with those that mourn" and "bear one another's burdens" (Mosiah 18:8–9) if we don't listen to know what those burdens are?

We discover and develop our thoughts through conversation. Talking itself is a sorting and learning process. We feel such comfort when others listen with the understanding that our words are not our final statement but a wondering and wandering process used to reach a clearer understanding.

But we must be careful not to listen as Laman and Lemuel listened to each other. They encouraged mutual murmuring. When fellow ward members complain, blame others, and repeat negative tales, it takes self-discipline to stop ourselves from adding more fuel to their fire of disgruntlement. Mutual murmuring is a smoldering fire that can burst into flame and destroy a ward.

Third, ward families provide encouragement. Becky and Danny's second child was born prematurely. Recounting the days, then weeks and years, of caring for a critically ill child, Becky says, "It was difficult for my mother to watch us dealing with this situation. She wished that she could take it away from me. We were living in a distant state, and Mother would call me on the phone and feel so helpless as she listened to our daily struggles. One day she said to me,

'Becky, I don't know how you will get through this, but I am confident that you can.' That encouragement was a turning point for me."

As a ward family, we can give the kind of encouragement that Becky's mother gave.

When friends express confidence in me, especially when I feel overwhelmed by difficult circumstances, the light at the end of the tunnel burns brighter. A steady belief in ward members can often be of far more value than casseroles or loaves of bread.

A mother was busily preparing dinner when her little boy burst into the kitchen. "Mother, will you play darts with me?" "Just-a-minutes" didn't seem to satisfy the little boy, so the mother followed him down the basement stairs. As they came into the playroom, she said, "I don't know the rules or how to play." "Oh, it's not hard at all," he beamed confidently. "I just stand right here and throw the darts, and you stand over there and say, 'Wonderful! Wonderful!'" Pretty easy rules to remember, aren't they?

"Wonderful, wonderfuls," notes, handshakes, hugs—all work so well in ward settings. Positive reinforcement changes behavior for the better, while criticism stabilizes negative behaviors and blocks change.

George Eliot, a nineteenth-century English novelist, said, "What do we live for, if it is not to make life less difficult to each other?" (*Middlemarch* [London: Penguin Books, 1965], p. 789.) We can make life less difficult for each other as we make our wards emotionally safer places: by being kind, accepting, tolerant, supportive, and positive. Those of us who teach children and youth have a special responsibility to insist—in respectful and kind ways—that class members use language and behavior that show respect for others. No one should be belittled or made to feel less than he is within the walls of a Church classroom.

Ward families are a refuge. I know a young family who lived in south Los Angeles during the violent summer of

1992. They could feel the heat from the fires as they sat terrified in their little apartment. They telephoned their parents in Salt Lake. Their families offered encouragement and their prayers. They could do no more at such a distance. It was a ward member who made arrangements for the Parkins to get themselves and their baby out safely. They stayed with members until they could go back to their apartment. They were safe.

Multiply this story by every natural and civil crisis. Bishops and quorum leaders accounting for families after hurricanes, members carrying food and blankets—it makes no difference where you live or what kind of chaos might occur, The Church of Jesus Christ of Latter-day Saints *will* remain organized, and order *will* prevail. The wards and stakes of Zion will be a "refuge from the storm." (D&C 115:6.)

Ward families provide ways for us to contribute. There are no boundaries for contributing our time and talents. Hopefully, we will contribute everywhere we go, but the structure of a ward provides a good training ground.

After living for twenty years in the same ward, I married and moved to a distant city, where my husband continued his schooling. The people were friendly, but I was shy by nature and struggled to feel comfortable. One Sunday morning as I stood up from the bench at the back of the chapel and turned to go to Sunday School, a member of the bishopric greeted me with a smile and a handshake. Brother Goates was one of many who had extended themselves in becoming acquainted with us. As he shook my hand, he said, "Virginia, get off the back row and join the congregation!"

All at once, I saw with a new perspective. He was right. I realized that I hadn't joined the congregation because I was consumed with thinking about myself. However, as the weeks moved on, the acceptance of a calling automatically moved me off the back row, demanding that I think about someone besides myself. My comfort and confidence grew proportionately. Callings and assignments are easy ways to become involved in the lives of others. Paradoxically, as we concentrate on the needs of others, our own needs become less controlling.

Ward families provide a laboratory to learn and practice the gospel. A CTR B teacher taught a lesson on fasting. After talking with their parents, she arranged for the children to visit Brother Dibble, a ward member who was very ill. As they visited, Sister McRae explained that their class had learned in Primary about fasting. Most of the children had never fasted before, and it was their desire, as a class, to fast and pray for Brother Dibble on the following fast Sunday. With tears rolling down his cheeks, he expressed in tender words his gratitude—for them, the gospel, and the principle of fasting. On Sunday, having fasted, Sister McRae and her class members knelt together in their classroom to pray for Brother Dibble and conclude their fast.

I have always believed that if people are really going to learn something, they need more than an explanation; they need an experience. Alma taught that principle as he encouraged experimenting upon the word. (See Alma 32:27.) Sister McRae's CTR B children received both an explanation and an experience. They learned and practiced the doctrine of fasting in a wonderful laboratory of gospel learning—their ward.

Like Sister McRae's CTR B class, young women are taught gospel principles during their Sunday lesson time. Then they are invited to "experiment on the word" by participating in Value experiences found in their *Personal Progress* books—the same process: an explanation and then an experience.

Heavenly Father expects us to participate in our wards. It is part of the plan. But, Sister Pearce, you may be saying, you have such an idealistic picture of a ward—that's not like *my* ward!

You mean, your ward has real people in it—ones who are selfish or self-righteous, unskilled, or undependable? I'm so glad! How could it be a *real* laboratory for practicing gospel principles like patience, long-suffering, charity, and forgiveness if there were no people or situations that would require the use of these principles? The miracle of it all is that we *are* real people put into an ingenious structure, designed by God, to help us become like Him.

I would invite you to love whatever ward you are in— participate in it, enjoy it, learn from it.

Each of us can envision our ward or branch as a Zion community and then work to make it that way.

I bear witness that ward and branch families are a great and miraculous part of Heavenly Father's plan. May we use them more fully to help us grow and ultimately return to His presence.

From an address given at the October 1993 general conference while Sister Pearce was serving as first counselor in the Young Women General Presidency. (See *Ensign*, Nov. 1993, pp. 79–81.)

Families

ELDER ROBERT B. HARBERTSON

May I introduce my remarks with two questions: what is your relationship with your parents, and, for those of you who are married, what is your relationship with your companion and your children? Now, think seriously about these questions for a moment. Are you comfortable with your thoughts and feelings? Do pride and joy start to swell within your heart? Or is there a tinge of resentment or guilt or even fear?

I remember one missionary who had just arrived in the mission field. He stood to bear his testimony, but no testimony was expressed. Instead, he dwelled on how much he hated his father and how he disliked being in his home. He said the only reason he had gone on a mission was to get away from his parents. My heart almost broke, I felt so sorry for this young elder. I wondered what had caused such feelings and what had gone wrong in his home. It just didn't seem fair, no matter where the fault might lie.

It made me reflect back to my home, my parents, and what my feelings were at that age. Oh, how blessed I was to have parents who loved me—yes, who loved me enough to guide me, direct me, and even discipline me when necessary. My feelings of love and security were so strong for my parents and home that when it came time to choose which basketball scholarship I should take (and I had been offered several full-ride scholarships), I picked the one that was closest to home!

The scriptures reveal some beautiful family relationships

that help to guide and strengthen all of us. In the book of Ruth we read of the great love and devotion a young woman had for her husband's mother. The husbands of Naomi and her daughters-in-law had died, leaving them alone. Naomi decided to return to her home in Bethlehem and suggested that the two daughters return to their own people. After some discussion, one of the daughters, Orpah, went her way, but Ruth clave unto her mother-in-law. Naomi said:

"Behold, thy sister in law is gone back unto her people, and unto her gods: return thou after thy sister in law.

"And Ruth said, Intreat me not to leave thee, or to return from following after thee: for whither thou goest, I will go; and where thou lodgest, I will lodge: thy people shall be my people, and thy God my God:

"Where thou diest, will I die, and there will I be buried: the Lord do so to me, and more also, if ought but death part thee and me." (Ruth 1:15–17.)

What a choice relationship. Naomi helped Ruth to capture the heart of Boaz, a mighty man of wealth. Through their marriage Ruth bore Obed, and Obed begat Jesse, who was the father of King David.

There must have been great love and trust in the family of Abraham, Sarah, and Isaac. I have tried to comprehend the awful task the Lord gave to Abraham when He said, "Take now thy son, thine only son Isaac, whom thou lovest, and get thee into the land of Moriah; and offer him there for a burnt offering upon one of the mountains which I will tell thee of." (Genesis 22:2.) I'm afraid I find it impossible to comprehend. My love and respect and admiration for Abraham are overwhelming. His testimony of the gospel and love for our Heavenly Father must have been pure and without blemish. I have tried to picture Abraham and his son as they made their trek to the mountain with their arms over each other's shoulders as I have done with my sons on many occasions. What emotion must have filled Abraham's being as he followed God's command. What love, faith, and trust Isaac must have had in his father as he said:

"My father: and he said, Here am I, my son. And he said, Behold the fire and the wood: but where is the lamb for a burnt offering?

"And Abraham said, My son, God will provide himself a lamb for a burnt offering: so they went both of them together. [Even at this point Abraham could not bring himself to tell his son what was to happen.]

"And they came to the place which God had told him of; and Abraham built an altar there, and laid the wood in order, and bound Isaac his son, and laid him on the altar upon the wood.

"And Abraham stretched forth his hand, and took the knife to slay his son." (Genesis 22:7–10.)

The test had been met; God's will meant more to both than mortal fears and desires. What love and understanding Abraham and Sarah had taught their mighty son, Isaac, who was spared to become a mighty man unto God.

What a thrill it must have been for Shiblon to hear the words of his father, Alma, to know of the faith and trust he had in him, and the love and pride his father felt for him as he said:

"And now, my son, I trust that I shall have great joy in you, because of your steadiness and faithfulness unto God; for as you have commenced in your youth to look to the Lord your God, even so I hope that you will continue in keeping his commandments; for blessed is he that endureth to the end.

"I say unto you, my son, that I have had great joy in thee already, because of thy faithfulness and thy diligence, and thy patience and thy long-suffering among the people of the Zoramites.

"For I know that thou wast in bonds; yea, and I also know that thou wast stoned for the word's sake; and thou didst bear all these things with patience because the Lord was with thee; and now thou knowest that the Lord did deliver thee." (Alma 38:2–4.)

What a great father-son relationship existed between them.

How pleased and proud our Father in Heaven must have been as He introduced His Son, Jesus Christ, to the Nephites. What a noble and valiant Son. Such a caring and loving Father. What great meaning in His words, "Behold my Beloved Son, in whom I am well pleased, in whom I have glorified my name—hear ye him." (3 Nephi 11:7.)

Are we creating such relationships with our parents and children? Are our priorities in order? Is there anything in the world more precious or eternal than families? Can greater joy or security be experienced than that felt within a family? I fear in some cases we allow the natural man or woman to overshadow the real treasures in life.

As a mission president, I was amazed to find out how few of our missionaries had truly experienced love, warmth, and understanding in their homes. It seemed to be the exception rather than the rule that a missionary could give and accept love freely. It had not been taught or experienced in their homes. I had grown up in a home where I loved, hugged, and kissed my dad freely. It had meant so much to me that I decided I would end interviews with each missionary with a warm handshake and an expression of love.

I couldn't believe the reactions I got. Some just melted, some stood as rigid as boards, and others didn't know how to react or what to do. They had never experienced such an expression of love from their dad in their whole life.

One elder who came to us had the sourest look on his face that I had ever seen. He would come in for each interview and sit down with the same unhappy expression. I would say, "What's the matter, Elder? Why don't you ever smile?"

I could never get an answer out of him. We would have

a poor interview, and at the end we would stand and I would extend my hand to him and tell him I loved him. I could almost see him shudder with disgust.

This went on for several months. He was a most unhappy young man. He had no success in his areas. He had companionship problems. Nothing went well.

Finally he came in for another interview. I said, "What's the matter, Elder? Can't you tell me?"

He looked at me for a moment, and then he said, "You want to know what's the matter? I'll tell you."

I thought, Great! We're finally going to get to the bottom of this thing.

He said, "I can't stand you."

I could have wished for a lot of other answers besides that one.

He continued, "I can't stand to have you tell me you love me. No one has ever told me that, not even my mother and dad, and I have never told anyone I loved them."

He was really rolling now. The floodgates were wide open. I was wondering why I had ever asked him the question.

He said, "I had a seminary teacher that was just like you. All the kids loved him, and I hated him."

I didn't know what to say. To be told you're hated isn't necessarily the greatest thing to hear. Finally I said, "Well, Elder, I'm really sorry I offend you, and I'm sorry it bothers you so for me to tell you I love you. I promise I will never again tell you I love you, but I want you to know that I truly do."

We stood up, we shook hands, and out the door he went. No more I love yous.

Finally it came time for Sister Harbertson and me to return home. I felt I had totally failed this elder. He came in for my final interview with him, and it went much as the others had gone. At last, we got up, we shook hands, and he walked to the door. Then he stopped, turned around, and said, "President Harbertson, I want you to know that I love you."

I nearly fainted. Later that day he got up in zone conference and for the first time in his whole life expressed love—first for his companion and then for Sister Harbertson and me.

Now, why did that young man have to go through twenty years of not feeling loved or giving love? It isn't fair or right. Good homes are so important.

Sons and daughters, are you really putting forth the effort to be close to your parents? Do you really know them and understand them? Parents, do you know your children? Are you enjoying each phase of their lives and being a strong influence for good?

The greatest influence in a child's life is his parents. Attitudes and personalities are greatly affected by this relationship. In the Doctrine and Covenants we read, "And that wicked one cometh and taketh away light and truth, through disobedience, from the children of men, and because of the tradition of their fathers." (D&C 93:39.)

As this verse points out, the traditions of our fathers, the way we act, the things we do and say, seem to influence our children significantly. Will you be happy if your children follow in your footsteps? Are you as children being obedient to God's way of life so that you may enjoy the strength and direction of the Holy Ghost?

Each experience and stage of life are precious moments, for they are lived only once. As Elder Richard L. Evans said:

"Those who are overly impatient for the future may let the happiness and opportunities, and also the obligations of the present, pass them by.

" . . . Happiness [is a matter] of learning to 'respect . . . the present hour' . . . learning to live each day. . . .

"This is our time, our day, . . . and we had better learn to live and 'labor while it is called today,' being mindful of each day's opportunities and obligations." (*Thoughts for One*

Hundred Days [Salt Lake City: Publishers Press, 1966], p. 129.)

President Spencer W. Kimball once said: "Fathers, what is your report concerning your family? Will you be able to report that you created an environment in your home to build faith in a living God, to encourage learning, to teach order, obedience, and sacrifice? That you often shared your testimony of the reality of your Father in heaven, of the truthfulness of the restored gospel with your wife and children? Will you be able to report that you followed the living prophets? That your home was where your tender children could feel protected and safe, and where they felt the love and acceptance and warmth of you and their mother?" (*Ensign,* June 1975, p. 7.)

First, it appears that an accounting must take place—we must report on our stewardship as a father, mother, husband, wife, son, or daughter. With a listening ear our Lord will judge our lives.

Obviously, teaching faith in God and obedience to His commandments is of prime importance. I'm particularly interested in President Kimball's question about the children and whether home is a place where they feel protection, safety, love, and warmth.

As a boy I had—and still do have, in fact—a great fear of the dark. I understand why the scriptures relate darkness to that which is not good. My biggest challenge day after day as a boy was going to bed each night, because I had to turn out the light and then get clear across the room and into bed before a monster could get me. I knew that monsters were in the closet and under the bed and behind the curtains. I got so I would start to run, hit the light, take one step inside the room, and then take a huge leap and hit the bed—most of the time. Mother never did know why the springs were broken on that side of the bed. Once I was in bed, up would go the covers over my head, and there I would lie paralyzed until I went to sleep.

Invariably I woke up in the middle of the night and fig-ured for sure I was a goner. Finally, when I just couldn't stand it any longer, I would throw back the covers and leap out of bed so the monsters under the bed couldn't grab me, race past the closet that always had a couple of monsters in it, and run down the hall to Dad and Mother's bedroom. That hall seemed as long as a football field. It was really only about ten feet long, but I had to go past the bathroom, the door to the kitchen, and the door to the living room, and you know who was lurking at each of them.

Once in the bedroom I could see my dad's big arm lift the bed covers into the air, and I would jump in beside him. Down would come the covers and his arm over me. Then I knew there wasn't a monster in the world big enough to get me. I have often wondered what would have happened if one night my dad had said, "Bobby, you big baby, get back in your own bed!" I'm afraid it would have caused perma-nent damage. But he didn't say it. He loved me, and he understood my fear. I knew that I was safe and secure in the arms of my dad and that he would never turn me away.

Are you enjoying the warmth and security and love of your parents? Do you counsel with them? Are you sharing precious experiences with them? Do you listen to them? When you return home, can they see and feel and hear of your love for them? Are you too big to hug and kiss them now? Remember, one day they will be gone.

I lost my dad, very unexpectedly, when I was only thirty-one. I had thought my dad would live forever. He was too big, too strong, to die; he was my hero; and yet without warning he was gone. Though I was married and had chil-dren of my own, I missed him so much. I craved to have him hold me once again. Please live each day so that you will not have regrets, no matter what may happen.

Love is such a special feeling. It brings so much joy and meaning to life. Those who radiate love truly enjoy the

Spirit of God. One of my favorite verses in the scriptures is this:

"A new commandment I give unto you, That ye love one another: as I have loved you, that ye also love one another.

"By this shall all men know that ye are my disciples, if ye have love one to another." (John 13:34–35.)

Is not the home where we learn to love, where we are first loved and made to feel secure and important? On the wall in our family room is a plaque that has these words written on it: "The greatest gift a father can give his children is to love their mother."

Nothing is more beautiful or reassuring than the eternal love between a husband and wife. That kind of love gives to our own children joy, security, strength, respect, and a desire to have the same kind of loving, eternal relationship. One of my favorite love stories brings out this kind of love, and it's a true one.

The nineteenth-century Irish poet Thomas Moore was called away on a business trip not long after he was married. Upon his return some weeks later, he was met at the door by the family doctor, who told him that his wife had contracted smallpox, which had left her once-flawless skin pocked and scarred. She had taken one look at her reflection in the mirror and ordered that the shutters be drawn and that her husband be forbidden to see her ever again.

Moore refused to listen. He ran to his wife's darkened room and threw open the door. Groping along the wall, he felt for the gas jets.

A startled cry came out of the darkness. "No! Don't light the lamps."

Moore hesitated, stopped by the pleading in her voice.

"Go!" she begged. "Please go! This is the greatest gift I can give you now."

Moore did go—down to his study, where he sat up most of the night, prayerfully writing. He had never written a song before, but now he wrote not only words but music, too. As soon as the sun came up, he returned to his wife's room.

"Are you awake?" he asked.

"Yes," came a voice from the darkness. "But you must not ask to see me, Thomas."

"I will sing to you, then," he said.

> Believe me, if all those endearing young charms
> Which I gaze on so fondly today,
> Were to change by tomorrow and fleet in my arms,
> Like fairy-gifts fading away,
> Thou would'st still be adored as this moment thou art,
> Let thy loveliness fade as it will,
> And around the dear ruin each wish of my heart
> Would entwine itself verdantly still.

As the last note of Moore's song faded away, his wife rose from her bed, crossed the room to the window, and slowly drew open the shutters. (See Galen Drake, *Guideposts*, Sept. 1957.)

I have yet to see a relationship that is not greatly enhanced when sensitive love and understanding are expressed by a husband to his wife. To a great extent the attitude and feelings one experiences through the day are generated by the atmosphere and environment felt in the home. Happiness, with all that is attached to it, is what we all desire and hope for. And yet, quite often, we seem to do and say things that are contrary and in exact opposition to happiness.

There is a simple but very important law taught time after time in the scriptures called the law of the harvest. Simply stated, it is this: "As ye sow, so shall ye reap." (See Galatians 6:7.) I don't believe it is ever more true than in a family relationship. The more one does for one's mate, children, parents, or brothers and sisters, the more one will receive in return. Good stimulates and nourishes good. The Lord expressed this truth most beautifully when he said:

"Fear not to do good, my sons, for whatsoever ye sow, that shall ye also reap: therefore, if ye sow good ye shall also reap good for your reward.

"Therefore, fear not, little flock: do good: let earth and hell combine against you, for if ye are built upon my rock, they cannot prevail." (D&C 6:33–34.)

May God bless each one of us to do all in our power to make our homes and relationships as parents, companions, and children special and to invite the Spirit of the Lord to help and direct us as we prepare for eternal life together as families.

From a fireside address given at Brigham Young University on 2 June 1985 while Elder Harbertson was serving as a member of the Seventy. (See *BYU 1984–85 Devotional and Fireside Speeches* [Provo, Utah: Brigham Young University Press, 1985], pp. 128–35.)

Great Shall Be the Peace
of Thy Children

E L D E R   M .   R U S S E L L   B A L L A R D

Little children, said our Lord and Savior, Jesus Christ, are "holy." (D&C 74:7.) I learned of the holy nature of little children when my wife, Barbara, gave birth to our first child, Clark. In those days, hospitals rarely allowed fathers in the delivery room to witness the birth. When Barbara was ready to deliver, a nurse sent me to the waiting room to pace and fret until she came out to tell me that mother and child were healthy and well.

That was an exciting moment—just as it was when each of our five daughters was born. I didn't think I could possibly have a greater feeling than when I heard the nurse say, "Mr. Ballard, you have a new daughter"—or son—followed by, "Your wife and the baby are both just fine."

Then our last child, Craig, was born. By this time hospitals encouraged a father to be in the delivery room with his wife when their child was born. Witnessing the miracle of birth was very impressive to me. I don't think I will ever forget the feeling I had when Craig was placed in my arms moments after his birth. I looked into his scrunched-up little face, and I could not help wondering what this spirit son of God could tell us if only he could speak.

Can anyone witness the miracle of birth and not feel a divine, providential influence? Can anyone look into the face of a precious newborn child and not see etched in its tiny lines and creases the confluence of eternity with mortality?

Perhaps that is one reason why the Savior tearfully urged His Nephite followers to "behold your little ones." (3 Nephi 17:23.) Notice that He didn't say "glance at them" or "casually observe them" or "occasionally take a look in their general direction." He said to behold them. To me that means that we should embrace them with our eyes and with our hearts; we should see and appreciate them for who they really are: spirit children of our Heavenly Father, with divine attributes.

When we truly behold our little ones, we behold the glory, wonder, and majesty of God, our Eternal Father. All children are His spirit offspring. We have no more eloquent testimony that our Heavenly Father lives and that He loves us than the first raspy cry of a newborn child. All babies have faith in their eyes and purity in their hearts. They are receptive to the truth because they have no preconceived notions; everything is real to children. Regardless of physical limitations or the challenge of circumstance, their souls are endowed naturally with divine potential that is infinite and eternal.

Jesus showed His great love and respect for children when His disciples asked Him this probing question: "Who is the greatest in the kingdom of heaven?

"And Jesus called a little child unto him, and set him in the midst of them,

"And said, Verily I say unto you, Except ye be converted, and become as little children, ye shall not enter into the kingdom of heaven.

"Whosoever therefore shall humble himself as this little child, the same is greatest in the kingdom of heaven.

"And whoso shall receive one such little child in my name receiveth me.

"But whoso shall offend one of these little ones which believe in me, it were better for him that a millstone were hanged about his neck, and that he were drowned in the depth of the sea." (Matthew 18:1–6.)

During one encounter with children during His mortal ministry, Jesus "took them up in his arms, put his hands upon them, and blessed them." (Mark 10:16.) On another occasion, "he took a child, and set him in the midst of them: and . . . [took] him in his arms." (Mark 9:36.) But nothing in recorded scripture rivals the beauty and intimacy of His tender ministry to the Nephite children in the land Bountiful:

"He took their little children, one by one, and blessed them, and prayed unto the Father for them.

"And when he had done this he wept again;

"And he spake unto the multitude, and said unto them: Behold your little ones.

"And as they looked to behold they cast their eyes towards heaven, and they saw the heavens open, and they saw angels descending out of heaven as it were in the midst of fire; and they came down and encircled those little ones about, and they were encircled about with fire; and the angels did minister unto them." (3 Nephi 17:21–24.)

Clearly, those of us who have been entrusted with precious children have been given a sacred, noble stewardship, for we are the ones God has appointed to encircle today's children with love and the fire of faith and an understanding of who they are.

How can they know of these most important matters unless we teach them? According to the scriptures, parents should teach children "that all men, everywhere, must repent, or they can in nowise inherit the kingdom of God." (Moses 6:57.) Children should learn "to pray, and to walk uprightly before the Lord" (D&C 68:28) and "to walk in the ways of truth and soberness; . . . to love one another, and to serve one another" (Mosiah 4:15). Our children should know "to what source they may look for a remission of their sins" (2 Nephi 25:26), and they should learn that they are to "love the Lord thy God with all thine heart, and with all thy soul, and with all thy might" (Deuteronomy 6:5).

Quoting Isaiah, the Savior told the Nephites: "And all thy children shall be taught of the Lord; and great shall be the peace of thy children." (3 Nephi 22:13.)

Peace. What a marvelous, desirable blessing to bring to the souls of our children. If they are at peace within themselves and secure in their knowledge of Heavenly Father and His eternal plan for them, they will be able to cope better with the unrest in the world around them and be prepared better for reaching their divine potential.

But how do we bring that peace into the lives of children who are growing up in trying, troubling times? Let us review what we can do as Church members. The best and most meaningful resources are found within the home where faithful, devoted parents and supportive brothers and sisters love one another and teach one another of their divine nature. Unfortunately, we live in a time when home and family values are under constant attack by Satan and his minions. We must ever recognize the significant and irreplaceable role of parents. Church leaders and teachers must support parents and teach them to fortify the home as a safe haven for their children. Allow me to suggest three ways that Church leaders and members can help bring peace and understanding to the children of God.

First suggestion: Bishops, you need to assert yourselves as the father of the ward. Parents are accountable for teaching their children and rearing them in righteousness, but bishops are responsible for the spiritual and temporal welfare of every person, including children, who lives within their ward boundaries.

Of course, you bishops are not alone in this stewardship. You have counselors and a ward council to assist in following the Savior's admonition to "bring up your children in light and truth." (D&C 93:40.) Is the Primary led by capable and loving leaders and teachers? Does a member of the bishopric meet regularly with the Primary presidency to teach them and listen to their concerns? Are calls to serve in the Primary being extended with dignity and without apology to emphasize the importance of ministering to the children? Do Primary leaders and teachers in your ward feel loved, respected, and appreciated? Do they have the vision that all children, active and less active, member and nonmember, within the ward boundaries need to be loved and invited to learn about Jesus and His gospel? Are you and your counselors finding ways to be personally involved with the children? Does the Primary get a fair share of the ward budget? Does one of you attend Primary meetings regularly to know firsthand how the children are nurtured and taught?

Some years ago when I was serving as a bishop, seven-year-old Danny got into some trouble with his teacher. He had been acting up regularly, and his teacher tried everything she could think of to prevent him from being so disruptive in class. Finally, she brought him to me. "Here's one of your flock, Bishop," she said. "Tend it!"

Danny and I sat in the bishop's office looking at each other for a few minutes. Then I said:

"We're going to work this out, Danny. Here's how we're going to do it. Every week after your class I want you to check with me and let me know how you got along in class. We're going to have a chance to become really good friends."

And that's just what happened. For the next couple of months, Danny met with me every week after his class, and we did become good friends. Knowing he would report on his behavior to me made a difference, and before very long he was able to behave himself without a weekly interview with his bishop.

Bishops, if you will listen and respond to the whisperings of the Holy Spirit, you will be guided to similar opportunities to bless the children entrusted to your care and keeping.

Second suggestion: Leaders and teachers need to focus more attention on the children. They cannot provide for themselves, so we need to join forces to provide for them. During presidency, leadership, and council meetings, spend less time planning, coordinating, and correlating and more time addressing the specific spiritual needs of individuals and families. Creative, innovative sharing times and quarterly activities can be stimulating and fun, but they don't mean much if the children are not there or if they come away having been entertained but not really enlightened, taught the gospel, or lifted spiritually. Teachers need to make sure that they are not simply preparing to teach a lesson but rather preparing to teach a child of God. Every lesson, every meeting, and every activity should be focused on bringing these little ones to Christ.

Often, they must be brought quite literally. I remember serving as an Aaronic Priesthood adviser for thirty-six boys. One youngster had a hard time making it to church. For many months I called him every Sunday morning and picked him up for priesthood meeting. That did not require much of my time. It did not take me away from my family. But it sent a powerful and important message to a young man that he was important, that somebody cared. Similarly, our leaders and teachers need to get involved in positive, meaningful ways with the children they have been called to serve.

Third suggestion: Remember, every individual child of God is equally important to Him. His love is not predicated upon membership in the Church. His love for His children knows no bounds and is absolutely unconditional. Likewise, our loving service to His children should be freely and fully extended to each child. An assignment to teach a class of one is just as significant as an assignment to teach a class of thirty-six. The one child who does not attend deserves our time and attention as much as those who do. The needs of children of other faiths in our communities merit our consideration regardless of their attitudes or feelings toward the Church.

Also, we must teach our own children to love and appreciate children of other faiths. In other words, our love and service should be extended to all children everywhere. Find them and invite them, love them without reservation, and serve them because they are all children of God and because doing so is simply the right thing to do.

May we move forward in powerful, positive ways to extend the love of God unconditionally to all of His children. Only then can we feel as the Savior did just before He blessed the little Nephite children: He said, "Behold, my joy is full." (3 Nephi 17:20.) We can share the feeling of the beloved Apostle John when he said, "I have no greater joy than to hear that my children walk in truth." (3 John 1:4.)

From an address given at the satellite broadcast "Behold Your Little Ones," 23 January 1994, while Elder Ballard was serving as a member of the Quorum of the Twelve Apostles. (See *Ensign*, Apr. 1994, pp. 59–61.)

Honour Thy Father and Thy Mother

Elder Dallin H. Oaks

Thousands of years ago, on a mountain near the Arabian peninsula, the Lord God of Israel gave His people ten commandments. The fifth commandment that the Lord gave through the prophet Moses was "Honour thy father and thy mother: that thy days may be long upon the land which the Lord thy God giveth thee." (Exodus 20:12.)

The commandment to honor our parents has strands that run through the entire fabric of the gospel. It is inherent in our relationship to God our Father. It embraces the divine destiny of the children of God. This commandment relates to the government of the family, which is patterned after the government of heaven.

The commandment to honor our parents echoes the sacred spirit of family relationships in which—at their best—we have sublime expressions of heavenly love and care for one another. We sense the importance of these relationships when we realize that our greatest expressions of joy or pain in mortality come from the members of our families.

Other manifestations of this commandment include the bearing and care of children, the preparation of family histories, and efforts to see that the ordinances of eternity are performed for our departed ancestors.

The Savior reemphasized the importance of the fifth commandment during His ministry. He reminded the scribes and Pharisees that we are commanded to honor our father and our mother and that God had directed that whoever cursed father or mother should be put to death. (See Leviticus 20:9; Deuteronomy 21:18–21; Matthew 15:4; Mark 7:10.) In this day, failing to honor our parents is not a capital crime in any country of which I am aware. Nevertheless, the divine direction to honor our father and our mother has never been revoked. (See Mosiah 13:20; Matthew 19:19; Luke 18:20.)

Like many scriptures, this commandment has multiple meanings.

To young people, honoring parents is appropriately understood to focus on obedience, respect, and emulation of righteous parents. The Apostle Paul illuminated that focus when he taught, "Children, obey your parents in all things [I believe he meant all righteous things]: for this is well pleasing unto the Lord." (Colossians 3:20.)

President Spencer W. Kimball combined the ideas of obedience and emulation in these words:

"If we truly honor [our parents], we will seek to emulate their best characteristics and to fulfill their highest aspirations for us. No gift purchased from a store can begin to match in value to parents some simple, sincere words of appreciation. Nothing we could give them would be more prized than righteous living for each youngster." (*The Teachings of Spencer W. Kimball,* ed. Edward L. Kimball [Salt Lake City: Bookcraft, 1982], p. 348.)

Young people, if you honor your parents, you will love them, respect them, confide in them, be considerate of them, express appreciation for them, and demonstrate all of these things by following their counsel in righteousness and by obeying the commandments of God.

To persons whose parents are dead, honoring parents is likely to involve thoughts of family reunions, family histories, temple work, and commitment to the great causes in which departed parents spent their lives.

Middle-aged persons are likely to think of the commandment to honor our fathers and our mothers in terms of caring for aged parents. President Ezra Taft Benson has encouraged families "to give their elderly parents and grandparents the love, care, and attention they deserve." He said: "Remember, parents and grandparents are our responsibility, and we are to care for them to the very best of our ability. When the elderly have no families to care for them, priesthood and Relief Society leaders should make every effort to meet their needs in the same loving way." (*Ensign,* Nov. 1989, p. 6.)

Recent years have seen great increases in the numbers and percentage of older people in our population. A recent study estimated that in another ten years one-seventh of the population of the United States, about thirty-five million people, will be at least 65 years old. At that time, about five million citizens will be age 85 or older. (See *Deseret News,* 7 May 1990, p. C1.)

From time to time, Church leaders hear of grown children who seem to be good Latter-day Saints but are negligent or even maliciously indifferent in caring for their aged parents. Some have encouraged parents to distribute their property and then have put them away in institutions, sometimes with inadequate care and sometimes without regular visits and expressions of love from their children. I believe this was the kind of circumstance the Lord's spokesman, the prophet Isaiah, thundered against when he commanded, "Hide not thyself from thine own flesh." (Isaiah 58:7.)

The best way to care for the aged is to preserve their independence as long as possible. President Benson explained:

"Even when parents become elderly, we ought to honor them by allowing them freedom of choice and the opportunity for independence as long as possible. Let us not take away from them choices which they can still make. Some parents are able to live and care for themselves well into their advancing years and would prefer to do so. Where they can, let them.

"If they become less able to live independently, then family, Church, and community resources may be needed to help them. When the elderly become unable to care for themselves, even with supplemental aid, care can be provided in the home of a family member when possible. Church and community resources may also be needed in this situation." (*Ensign*, Nov. 1989, p. 7.)

When aged parents who are not able to live alone are invited to live with their children, this keeps them in the family circle and allows them to continue their close ties with all members of the family. When a parent lives with one child, the other children should make arrangements to share the burdens and blessings of that arrangement.

When it is not possible for parents to be cared for in the homes of their children, so that some type of institutional care is obtained, their children should remember that institutional care will generally focus on physical needs. Members of the family should make regular visits and contacts to provide the spiritual and emotional sustenance and the love that must continue in the family relationship for mortal life and throughout all eternity.

In some nations where our members reside, the obligation to care for aged parents is more keenly felt and more faithfully observed than in the United States. I saw this in Asia. But the care of aged parents is still a strongly felt obligation among most Americans. Six out of ten older persons questioned in a recent national survey had weekly personal visits with their children, and three-fourths of them talked on the telephone with their children at least weekly. Two-thirds of those surveyed expect to take care of their elderly parents. (See *Deseret News*, 7 May 1990, p. C1.)

Latter-day Saints have a good record of caring for their aged parents and for older citizens generally. I have seen wonderful examples of this in my own family and among my LDS friends and associates. Many of our General Authorities and their companions have been exemplary in caring for their aged parents.

When I was a young boy in a small Utah town, I remember seeing my grandmother overseeing the provision of food, favors, transportation, and entertainment for a large group of elderly in the community. As a counselor in the stake Relief Society presidency, she was making preparations for "Old Folks Day."

Most of you have never heard of Old Folks Day. It was a unique Utah Mormon institution. It began in 1875, when Charles R. Savage, the pioneer photographer, persuaded Presiding Bishop Edward Hunter to declare a day for honoring those we now call senior citizens. The first Old Folks Day transported guests by rail to an outing at Saltair, west of Salt Lake City. A monument honoring that celebration and its founder stands on the southeast corner of Temple Square.

The annual Old Folks Day celebrations were held in nearly every community in Utah. Travel, refreshments, and entertainment were given to all citizens seventy years of age and older. Although this holiday was conducted by the leaders and members of this Church, it was stipulated that "there are none to be excluded because of their religion, and the oldest guest present is the special guest of the occasion whether they be white or black or whatever the complexion of their religious belief." (Quoted in Joseph Heinerman, "The Old Folks Day: A Unique Utah Tradition," *Utah Historical Quarterly* 53 [Spring 1985]: 158.)

The committee directing these celebrations was dissolved in 1970, and the responsibility for honoring those who had come to be called senior citizens was passed to the stake presidents of the Church. Since that time we have had further increases in the number of senior citizens in our midst, but perhaps not significant increases in the amount of honor accorded them. Fortunately, the advances in medical science that have produced increased longevity have also increased our senior citizens' effective participation in church, community, business, and social events. But the need for honor, especially for our fathers and our mothers, is undiminished.

The fifth commandment is often referred to as the first commandment with a promise: "Honour thy father and thy mother: that thy days may be long upon the land which the Lord thy God giveth thee." (Exodus 20:12.) I have wondered about the relationship between the commandment and the promise. How could honoring our parents increase our longevity?

During almost forty years of marriage, I have observed something that provides at least a partial explanation of how this promise is fulfilled.

In the early days of our marriage, I spent many happy hours in the home of my wife's parents, Charles and True Dixon. There I met June's maternal grandmother, Adelaide White Call. Then a widow about eighty-five years of age, Grandma Call was a survivor of what older people called "the exodus." She had been among those valiant Latter-day Saints expelled from northern Mexico in 1912. Now her sons and daughters were living throughout the United States. In her later years, they helped her locate in Utah County, near June's parents.

During my visits, I saw the gentleness and love and concern with which the Call children and their companions looked after this older parent. They visited her frequently. My wife's mother looked in on her every day and often had her in their home. They made her part of every occasion in which she desired to participate, and they gave her every consideration and respect. They cared for her every need when she was ill. Surely, I said to myself, these Call children honor their mother.

It has been about forty years since I saw that honor given. Now I see its effects. I see June and her brother and sisters honoring their mother as they saw their mother honoring her own mother. Fortunately, True Dixon is blessed with good health and vigor and has no present need for the kind of care her mother required. Still, her children are attentive. There are frequent visits and phone calls and invitations that include her in all the family activities she desires. I believe her days will be longer upon the land because of the attentiveness and companionship of her children, who learned the way to honor a parent by seeing how their own mother honored hers.

I am grateful for this example and for this principle, especially when I anticipate the effect of having our daughters and sons observe how their mother honors her mother. I am sure that when the time comes, my own companion's days will be lengthened upon the land because of the care her children will give to her because of the example she has set for them. A worthy example repeats itself from generation to generation. Truly, righteousness is a beacon and a worthy act is its own reward. As the Lord said, "He who doeth the works of righteousness shall receive his reward, even peace in this world, and eternal life in the world to come." (D&C 59:23.)

In time to come, each of us will be judged by the Lord God of Israel, who commanded us to honor our fathers and our mothers. I pray that each of us will conduct ourselves toward our parents in such a way that we will be guiltless before God at that day.

From an address given at the April 1991 general conference while Elder Oaks was serving as a member of the Quorum of the Twelve Apostles. (See *Ensign,* May 1991, pp. 14–17.)

Just the Two of Us — for Now

SISTER ARDETH G. KAPP

My husband and I do not have any children at the present time. Our blessings in this matter have been delayed. But make no mistake, we are even now a family. Our family unit was established by the authority of God at the same time that we knelt at the altar in the temple. Children come as an extension and an expansion of the family. When a man and a woman are married, they immediately become a family and remain a family even in the temporary absence of children.

I mention this because I know many couples struggle with the sorrow of childlessness. I would like to share with those of you who have not been blessed with children my testimony and some of my insights gained from personal experience about our particular challenge.

Brother Kapp and I understand and remember some of the pains and much of the suffering that you suffer. We remember the emotional highs and lows with every month, including the fast and testimony meetings when testimonies were borne by those who asked in faith and were blessed with children. We know how you return home and put two dinner plates on the table and recall the marriage covenant to multiply and replenish the earth and your desperate desire to qualify for that honor in righteousness. You can't explain your feelings to each other, much less to your family and friends; and your whole soul cries out as did Job, "If I be righteous, . . . I am full of confusion; therefore see thou mine affliction." (Job 10:15.)

131

Some of you go through the suffering and concerns of
your childlessness year after year until finally you may
even say, "My soul is weary of . . . life" (Job 10:1), thinking
that if you have no children, you cannot fill the measure of
your creation. And if you don't fill the measure of your creation, you may say to yourselves, what else matters?

I will forever remember the day a child new to our neighborhood knocked on our door and asked if our children
could come out to play. I explained to him, as to others young
and old, for the thousandth time, that we didn't have any
children. This little boy squinted his innocent face in a quizzi-
cal look and asked the question that I had not dared put into
words: "If you are not a mother, then what are you?"

But then came the day my young husband was called to
be a bishop and I was finally convinced that our not having
children was not because of our unrighteousness. Some
don't understand that. A good man in the ward who had
desired that position came to him privately with strong
emotion and said, "What right do you have to be a bishop,
and what do you know about helping a family? Don't ever
expect me or my family to come to you for anything!" In
time my husband helped that man's family through a serious crisis, and through it we forged a lasting bond of love
with them.

You have undoubtedly had similar experiences. If you
haven't, you will. In these ways we grow from the time
when everything hurts and offends us until, with faith in
God, we are neither hurt nor offended. But I want you to
know I understand if you feel hurt or offended now.

Mother's Day may be one of those times of hurt. Every
year there will be a Mother's Day, and every year at church
a little plant or some other gift may be forced into your
clenched fist. But one day you will learn to open your heart,
and then, somehow, you will open your hand to receive that
gift. Eventually, that gift becomes the symbol of an eternal
promise.

I know a childless woman who, at the age of fifty-eight, went into the hospital for a hysterectomy. She couldn't handle the emotional impact of that event, and she wept bitter tears of anguish, saying, "Now I know that I'll never have any children." She and her husband lived together in loneliness, waiting, never facing reality and never able to make the adjustments that could have brought them a full life.

How do we handle unfulfilled expectations? First, we must accept the reality that this life is not intended to be free of struggle. In fact, it is through struggle that we are given opportunities to fulfill the very purpose of this mortal life. It is the fiery trials of mortality that will either consume us or refine us.

Part of those trials is facing alternatives and making decisions. For those of us without children, the choices may seem incredibly difficult to make. What would the Lord have us do? To what extent do we seek medical attention? What about adoption and foster children? What about no children? If that is the choice, then what do we do with our lives? The choices are never simple. During these times of searching, we often find ourselves caught between conflicting counsel from parents and friends and leaders and doctors and other experts. Some couples I've known even consider divorce, each one thinking the other is responsible.

From my own experience, I've learned that the only lasting peace is the peace that comes when we learn the Lord's will concerning our opportunities in life. To do that, we must consider our alternatives, formulate a decision, and take it to the Lord. Then, as Elder Dallin H. Oaks observed when he was president of Brigham Young University, "When a choice will make a real difference in our lives— . . . and where we are living in tune with the Spirit and seeking his guidance, we can be sure we will receive the guidance we need to attain our goal. The Lord will not leave us unassisted when a choice is important to our eternal welfare." (Devotional address, 29 Sept. 1981, in

Brigham Young University 1981–82 Fireside and Devotional Speeches [Provo: University Publications, 1982], p. 26.) I believe that. We just don't know the Lord's timeline, and that is where our faith comes in.

I have two younger sisters, both of whom are mothers. My youngest sister, Shirley, has eleven children. Sharon, another sister, has a little girl who was born to her after six years of anxious waiting. Ten years later, through the fervent prayers of the extended family for the wonderful blessing of adoption, a little boy came into their family and was sealed to them in the temple for time and eternity. What a blessing he and the other children have been to all of us!

Over the years my sisters and I, with our husbands, have prayed for each other and with each other and about each other. We have come to know that the Lord has answered our prayers differently and not always in the affirmative and not always according to our timeline. But we have all felt the warm assurance of His approval and love.

There will be times when you may feel that your desires are righteous but the answer is still no. At that point, the only way to peace is to say, "Not my will but thine be done." The Lord doesn't have to explain His decisions to us. If He did, how would we learn faith? I have learned that we must make our choices—even the hard ones—and then accept responsibility for the consequences. It is in facing the awesome responsibility of using our agency and, in faith, making decisions of great eternal consequence that we are drawn close to God.

Someday, maybe years after the trial of our faith, we will receive a witness that our decisions were right. (See Ether 12:6.) But until then, those who try to live in tune with the promptings of the Spirit must exercise no small degree of faith and courage in following that Spirit.

What, then, are some of the decisions couples can make to lead fulfilled lives when the answer is that they will not have children in this life? One night, as my husband and I were reaching for that kindly light to lead us 'mid the encircling gloom, we read from President David O. McKay, "The noblest aim in life is to strive . . . to make other lives . . . happier." (In Conference Report, Apr. 1961, p. 131.)

It was like a beacon in the dark. It became a motto, a guiding light. That night, speaking I think by inspiration from the Lord, the patriarch of our family said to me, "You need not possess children to love them. Loving is not synonymous with possessing, and possessing is not necessarily loving. The world is filled with people to be loved, guided, taught, lifted, and inspired."

My husband and I knew that parents are constantly placed in situations that develop unselfishness and sacrifice. We began to realize that if we were to learn the important lessons that our friends with children were learning, we needed to place ourselves in situations where we could serve and sacrifice. So we began to say yes to everything and to everyone.

It wasn't long before we had many opportunities to serve and sacrifice. Often, at the end of a long week we would plan for a moment together—just the two of us—and the telephone would ring. We'd postpone our moment together and carry on with joyful, grateful hearts for our opportunities, hoping to qualify even in some small measure for the quality spoken of by Elder Neal A. Maxwell:

"So often our sisters [and I would add brothers] comfort others when their own needs are greater than those being comforted. That quality is like the generosity of Jesus on the cross. Empathy during agony is a portion of divinity! . . . They do not withhold their blessings simply because some blessings are [for now at least] withheld from them." (*Ensign,* May 1978, pp. 10–11.)

We who do not have children can wallow in self-pity, or we can experience "birth pains" as we struggle to open the passageway to eternal life for ourselves and others. I bear testimony to you that instead of wrapping your empty and aching arms around yourself, you can reach out to others. As you do so, one day you will even be able to hold your friends' babies and rejoice. You will be able to rejoice with the mother of a new bride, and the mother of a newly called missionary, and even with your friends the day they become grandmothers. How can that be? Let me tell you.

We were alone with each other in St. George, Utah, one Thanksgiving time because all our relatives were with their families. It was early in the morning in the motel; the room was quiet, and I was thinking. I remember my heart crying out as I anticipated Christmas approaching. And although we could share in the joy and excitement of our nieces and nephews, it wasn't like having your own children with stockings to hang. The whole thing seemed to me to be unfair. I felt a darkness and a despondency settle over me, and I did what I'd learned to do over the years. I got on my knees and prayed for insight.

My answer came when I opened the scriptures to Doctrine and Covenants 88:67–68: "And if your eye be single to my glory [and remember, God's glory is to help 'to bring to pass the immortality and eternal life of man' (Moses 1:39)] your whole bodies shall be filled with light, and there shall be no darkness in you; and that body which is filled with light comprehendeth all things.

"Therefore, sanctify yourselves that your minds become single to God, and the days will come that ye shall see him; for he will unveil his face unto you, and it shall be in his own time, and in his own way, and according to his own will."

I don't know how long it will be for you. For us it was years. But one day you will gain an eternal perspective, and you will feel peace not pain, hope not despair. I would have liked so much to have received that insight years before, but I know that had that happened, I would have been deprived of the growth that comes from being comforted by the witness of the Spirit after the trial of my faith.

If I have any comforting message for you, it is this—Peace of mind comes from keeping an eternal perspective. Motherhood, I believe, is a foreordained mission. For some, this glorious blessing may be delayed, but it will not be denied. Motherhood is an eternal reality for all women who live righteously and accept the teachings of the gospel.

On the other hand, the characteristics of motherhood, which include concern for others, sacrifice, service, compassion, teaching, encouraging, and inspiring can be the noble labor for each one of us now, with or without children. The fate of each spirit in the eternities to come depends so much on the training it receives from those here and now who are willing to help another gain eternal life.

To participate in this glorious work gives meaning and purpose, great joy, and eternal blessings each and every day, even as we anticipate the promises of the future.

If you don't think that will be enough comfort, let me close with this thought by President Brigham Young:

"Let me here say a word to console the feelings . . . of all who belong to this Church. Many of the sisters grieve because they are not blessed with offspring. You will see the time when you will have millions of children around you. If you are faithful to your covenants, you will be mothers of nations. . . . and when you have assisted in peopling one earth, there are millions of earths still in the course of creation. And when they have endured a thousand million times longer than this earth, it is only as it were the beginning of your creations. Be faithful, and if you are not blest with children in this time, you will be hereafter." (In *Journal of Discourses*, 8:208.)

From a fireside address given 1 November 1981 at Brigham Young University and published while Sister Kapp was serving as Young Women General President. (See Ardeth Greene Kapp, *My Neighbor, My Sister, My Friend* [Salt Lake City: Deseret Book Co., 1990], pp. 122–28.)

Single Again

PRESIDENT JANETTE C. HALES

As I anticipated speaking tonight, I thought how much I would rather talk with each of you one-on-one. Although most of us gathered here are single, our experiences are so varied that a private setting might be a better way to share. We do, however, have much in common. Singly we were born into this world, and singly we will depart.

Single members include individuals in countless circumstances. Yet when we realize that about 35 percent of the adults in the Church are single, we shouldn't feel so different.

I became single again when I was quite suddenly widowed some years ago. I can speak only from my own experience, but I have learned a good deal, and I have a few pet peeves. For example, as a single person I can make up my mind to go to a banquet alone, but why don't they ever set a table for five or seven or nine? And who started the false notion that single people have twice as much time when they have to do everything for themselves? I relate to your frustration and occasional anger, for some of the experiences that have brought us together are painful. You have helped me and taught me. I have loved your letters, your humor, your courage, your patience. You are helping me understand your experiences. You are helping my love for the gospel to become deeper and richer.

While visiting my son one summer, I appreciated an interpretation a ward member related of the parable of the Good Samaritan. You remember in Luke that a certain lawyer had asked the Master what he must do to inherit eternal life. After being told, "Thou shalt love the Lord thy God with all thy heart . . . and thy neighbour as thyself," the man asked, "Who is my neighbour?" Jesus told of the man stripped of his raiment who was left wounded, even half dead. Those who might have helped passed him by. In this interpretation, the Good Samaritan who rendered service is our Savior, Jesus Christ. It was He who was unaccepted, even despised, by the Jewish people. We then are the wounded. He picks us up and ministers to our wounds and then takes us to an inn. He lingers long enough to be sure there are others to assume our care. He compensates the host for his effort. And then my favorite words: "Take care of him; and whatsoever thou spendest more, when I come again, I will repay thee." In other words, whatever it takes to help those in need, it is not too much and He will repay the debt.

Many of us have had a time in our lives when we felt stripped of our security, left alone, wounded. Many too can testify that in times of devastation, they feel surprisingly supported, even suspended in love. When that feeling of support starts to leave, it could be a letdown, but perhaps that can be a reminder that a time of healing is a temporary time and soon we need to start taking more responsibility for ourselves.

The inn is a wonderful symbol. It is a temporary place—a place of transition. How many of us want to take up permanent residence as a guest of life? But if we make that choice, we would not as likely realize our potential or reach that destination of eternal life. No matter what our past experience, it is important to realize that we must prepare to move on.

After a major change in our lives, the journey seems different, even dangerous. Perhaps loving, even trusting, others is too much risk. At one point, I felt my heart was so covered with Band-Aids that I feared I might bleed to death in public.

When my husband was a medical student, he told me of a wise professor who said to a group of interns, "Remember, you put the stitches in to close the wound, but you don't knit the skin together. The miracle of healing takes place from the inside out." In this sense, the inn is a caring environment where healing can take place. The healing is a miracle. This is a time when we are open to new spiritual insights. A friend wisely told me not to be afraid of the wide range of my emotions as they would enlarge my heart and my understanding. Gradually I have learned that experience, even difficult experience, can increase our appreciation and our ability to understand and to care.

As I resumed my journey as a single parent, I had to make some new decisions. For years while my children were growing up, I had boldly said to them, "I would never ever miss something that I really wanted to do just because I didn't have a date." Those words came back to haunt me. I remember so vividly the fall of 1988, less than six months after becoming a widow. The football stadium that had been so exciting and so friendly looked so big and so lonely. I felt like a child standing alone in a coliseum in a foreign country, but you know about those feelings. Perhaps there was a place that was hard for you.

After considering the alternatives, I made a conscious decision to live as generously and courageously as I could until this life is finished. I went to ball games. I decided to run for the state legislature. When I wavered, my daughter Karen said, "Mom, wouldn't you rather have people ask, 'How is your campaign going?' instead of, 'How is your grieving going?'" Her wise words kept *me* going.

As a single person, I am aware of couples holding hands as they journey forward. I miss that companionship. I often long for someone to care about who cares about me and what I care about as much as I care about him and what he cares about. But how much of life we waste wanting things to be other than how they are. What really matters most is what we are doing with what we have. How gratifying to learn that life can be happy and fulfilling even when our first choice is not one of the options. Staying in the inn is necessary at times, but much of our learning takes place as we move on and try to move closer to our Heavenly Father. There are some things that I understand better because of experience. In order to have a productive and responsible life, I know I must avoid the natural tendency to be selfish or to relish comfort. I must avoid the tendency when hurt to turn inward and become afraid to continue. I am learning to accept the fact that suffering and misfortune are a part of the human condition.

Each of us is at times in need, but we don't need to be counted among those who pass by the needy.

Progress involves work. There is some work, whether we are married or single, that each of us must do alone; but we can be grateful that we can also work together at times, and we can support one another. As we move on with our lives, we must learn to see ourselves honestly and be aware of obstacles that will hold us back. We cannot always progress according to the expectations of others. Occasionally that means slowing down to be sure our footing is secure and even to eliminate a little baggage. Carrying old hurts or disappointments may keep us from our destination.

Wherever any of us are at this time, could we begin to have greater appreciation for the gospel of Jesus Christ and the gift of peace that passeth our understanding? The "wisdom that is from above is first pure, then peaceable." (James 3:17.) I believe the joy that is available in this life is available to every man, woman, and child, for happiness is the "state of those that keep the commandments." (Mosiah 2:41.)

As we work to move forward and strengthen our lives, may we each in our own way become innkeepers—willing and able to do the work of the Master. What does He ask of us? That we love one another, as Paul taught the Corinthians, "that the members should have the same care one for another. And whether one member suffer, all the members suffer with it; or one member be honoured, all the members rejoice with it. Now ye are the body of Christ." (1 Corinthians 12:25–27.) I pray that this might be our common bond, that in this we may be single.

From an address given 30 August 1992 at a fireside for single adults while President Hales was serving as Young Women General President.

A Yearning for Home

ELDER MARVIN J. ASHTON

At some time in your life, you've probably experienced the pangs of homesickness. It might have been those first times you stayed overnight with a friend or went on a sleepover, as our grandchildren call them. As much as you wanted to be with your friends, you might have been lonely for your parents and for the secure feeling of being home, where it was safe and comfortable.

Sustained homesickness might not have come until later—when you left for college or to serve a mission, or even when you were uprooted by marriage and a move far from home. Or it might have occurred when your parents divorced and you found yourself struggling to adapt to new surroundings and maybe even a stepparent and new relatives. During these periods of adjustment and absence, you perhaps felt unsettled, lonely, and had a deep yearning for home.

Recently a mission president asked me to speak to a troubled missionary who was having extreme homesickness problems. His intense yearnings were causing poor performance, a waste of time, a lack of concentration, and a dislike for his present assignment. I took the occasion to tell him that some of the right kind of homesickness could be desirable, but it must be kept under control. Let me say at the outset, *yearning* is defined "to have a strong or deep desire; be filled with longing." This missionary seemed very sincere in wanting to do better. Proper yearnings for home can be beneficial.

Not just children but all of us will think of home under joyous or trying circumstances. We let ourselves become homesick for love, acceptance, security, understanding, and guidance that generally are taught and shared there. Home should be the place in which a person can unburden his soul and find renewed strength to face the world, where there is comfort, joy, and understanding, where best friends live, and where we can learn to be our best selves.

There is a certain kind of yearning for home we should never want to lose. Home should be an anchor, a port in a storm, a refuge, a happy place in which to dwell, a place where we are loved and where we can love. Home should be where life's greatest lessons are taught and learned. Home and family can be the center of one's earthly faith, where love and mutual responsibility are appropriately blended. Thinking of home with its pleasant and happy memories can make us stronger during our present and future days here upon the earth.

President Ezra Taft Benson has always loved his childhood home. He loves Whitney, Idaho, his birthplace. He loves the homestead where all eleven children were born and reared by noble parents.

Over a lifetime of worldwide travel, he yearned to return often to his home, and he did so. His heart has always been in Cache Valley. He loved going back and visiting with family members still there and seeing the friends of his birth, his neighbors, his teachers, his bishops, his kin who had such an impact for good on his life. He calls them "the finest people in all the world," and Whitney "the ideal farm community."

It revitalizes President Benson to go back to his roots, to go back to the land that nourished him and built character in him and provided him the sacred beginnings of a life devoted to God, family, and country. Truly, President Benson loves his childhood home.

I am concerned for people today who do not have a

longing for or thoughts of home. It is unfortunate that among us we have people who have never experienced home life that has been and is desirable so that there can be an anxiousness under control for thoughts toward home. Our responsibilities are to share the warmth of our homes by being good neighbors and friends.

To know who we are is important, but to know where we are in relationship to our earthly home and heavenly home is essential if we are to receive all the blessings our Father in Heaven has for those who love Him and keep His commandments. Our eternal home is our ultimate destination. A proper yearning for home can prevent our getting lost in detours or paths that lead us away.

It is reported that one summer at a Young Women's conference in Alberta, Canada, three hundred girls were camped in tents scattered among tall pines. It rained every day and was very cold and wet. Even so, there was no murmuring in the camp. The last day of the conference, the leader addressed the young women under cloudy skies. Despite the unseasonable cold, there was a feeling of warmth among them for this their temporary home. Maybe because of the cold, they were all drawn together and felt warm from the inside out.

The speaker began her remarks by asking, "Where are you going following this outdoor conference?" The united chorus of three hundred young women resounded through the tall pines. "Home!" they cried out. "Where?" they were asked again, and they responded with even greater conviction, "Home!" They knew where they wanted to go most of all and were anxious to get there.

The most attractive home that we will ever share will be that abode with our families with appropriate relationship to our Heavenly Father and His Son, Jesus Christ. Even the prodigal son could not resist the pull of home. He spurned his father, his home life, and his heritage, lavishly wasting his inheritance on riotous living. When he had nothing and was reduced to living off the spoils that only swine would eat, his thoughts turned homeward. Could there have been moments, as he gleaned the fields for husks to eat, when he longed for the security, safety, and acceptance he'd had before? Might he have been deeply homesick? Repentant, and hoping his father would accept him as a servant, he finally returned home. His father rejoiced, welcoming him back with open arms and complete acceptance. He no doubt knew that welcoming his wayward son was crucial if he hoped ever to return to his heavenly home. (See Luke 15:11–32.)

Over the years I've counseled with many whose homesickness threatened to interfere with their missions, marriages, and families.

But I've come to see that being homesick isn't all bad. It's natural to miss the people you are closest to. It's normal to long to be where you feel secure, where those you love have your best interests at heart. It's understandable to want to return to the place where you learned how to walk and talk, where you felt loved, even when friends turned away, and where you were accepted, regardless of the situation. There's no place on earth that can take the place of a home where love has been given and received.

Recently we witnessed the tragic devastation that Hurricane Andrew left in its wake in southern Florida and Louisiana. Tens of thousands of people have lost their homes. Armed forces personnel have raised tent cities to at least provide these victims with shelter. But the sobering fact is that, at least for a time, many of these people literally cannot go home. I cannot imagine how they must yearn for what they so recently had.

I have known other men and women who, for one reason or another, could not go home or who had no home to go to. I have felt their pain and seen their tears. It is, at best, a heartbreaking situation.

In another application, I have also known men and

women who have jeopardized the privilege of returning to their heavenly home. Some were dealing with problems that made them ineligible to enter the temple and make the eternal covenants that bind us to our eternal home. I have felt their heartache and their longing for opportunities that, at least for a time, were beyond their reach.

The ramifications are poignant and endless. Perhaps we've all had these overwhelming thoughts come to mind: What if I am unworthy? What if I could never go home?

If he could have his way, Satan would distract us from our heritage. He would have us become involved in a million and one things in this life—probably none of which are very important in the long run—to keep us from concentrating on the things that are really important, particularly the reality that we are God's children. He would like us to forget about home and family values. He'd like to keep us so busy with comparatively insignificant things that we don't have time to make the effort to understand where we came from, whose children we are, and how glorious our ultimate homecoming can be!

We are literally the children of our Heavenly Father. We kept our first estate. During our experience in premortality, we lived with and were cared for and taught by a loving Father. Among other things, we were schooled in what had to be a perfect spiritual and educational environment. And we rejoiced when told of the plan whereby we could prove ourselves. Hence the day arrived when it was our turn to experience a period of probation and testing, a period during which a veil would be drawn over our memories so that we would be free either to walk by faith and by the Spirit or to forsake our spiritual heritage and birthright.

Now we're here. And I'm sure we would all agree that this second estate has lived up to its billing. It is a time of testing, of probation. The challenges and duties and responsibilities, at times, seem to overshadow almost everything else. Sadly, it's easy to become so encumbered by the press of daily life that we lose our focus.

One definition of the word *focus* is "directed attention," or "emphasis." Perhaps as much as anything, in this day and age of mass media, instantaneous worldwide communications, and modern conveniences that seem to help us pack more into each day than would have been considered possible just a few decades ago, we need to focus and direct our attention on the things that really matter. And simply, what really matters is a personal testimony of Jesus Christ, an understanding of who we are and what we're doing here, and an absolute determination to return home.

What young musician, after years of agonizing rehearsal was finally scheduled to debut in a capacity concert hall, would, while en route to the performance, stop to join a long line forming at the latest hit movie, forgetting the thousands of people waiting to hear her?

What world-class runner, after training for well over a decade, would find himself in the Olympic finals, only to stop running halfway through his race to watch the high-jump finals taking place on the other side of the field?

These examples may seem preposterous—but how much more tragic that someone who, equipped with a testimony of the truth and a knowledge of the purpose of life, becomes more absorbed in life today than in life forever. Who's just a little more concerned about his or her status and standing in mortality than in eternity. Whose focus is not directed to God the Father and His Son, Jesus Christ, with whom it is possible to have a glorious connection and bond.

I fear that, at times, we run the risk of acting like seasoned, conditioned athletes who are more interested in what kind of jogging suits we'll wear than in buckling down to train for the race. C. S. Lewis had an intriguing way of evaluating this dilemma: "We are half-hearted creatures, fooling about with drink and sex and ambition when infinite joy is offered us, like an ignorant child who wants to go on making mud pies in a slum because he cannot imagine what is meant by the offer of a holiday at the sea. . . . We are far too easily pleased." (*A Mind Awake* [New York: Harcourt Brace Jovanovich, 1968], p. 168.)

The prophet Mormon put it another way: "Why are ye ashamed to take upon you the name of Christ? Why do ye not think that greater is the value of an endless happiness than that misery which never dies—because of the praise of the world?" (Mormon 8:38.)

When we have a yearning and don't know what it is for, perhaps it's our soul longing for its heartland, longing to be no longer alienated from the Lord and the pursuit of something much higher, better, and more fulfilling than anything this earth has to offer.

After Joseph, the next-to-youngest son of Jacob, had been reunited with his brothers, he asked them to return home to Canaan to bring his father, Jacob, to him in Egypt. As the brothers were preparing to depart, Joseph said to them simply, "See that ye fall not out by the way." (Genesis 45:24.)

Might our Heavenly Father have given us much the same counsel as we departed His presence to begin our earthly sojourn?

May our yearning for home be the motivation we need to so live that we can return to our heavenly home with God our Father on a forever basis.

From an address given at the October 1992 general conference while Elder Ashton was serving as a member of the Quorum of the Twelve Apostles. (See *Ensign,* Nov. 1992, pp. 21–23.)

Index